THE NORDIC COUNCIL

A Study of Scandinavian Regionalism

The Nordic Council

A STUDY OF
SCANDINAVIAN REGIONALISM

By Stanley V. Anderson

University of Washington Press   SEATTLE AND LONDON
The American-Scandinavian Foundation   NEW YORK

JN 7042 . A7 1967

This book is published with the assistance of a grant from Nordiska Kulturfonden.

TO MY FATHER AND MOTHER

FOREWORD

THIS BOOK is an attempt to describe and explain Scandinavian regionalism by illuminating its most prominent organ, the Nordic Council. Founded in 1952, the Council is an official consultative assembly of members of Parliament from Denmark, Finland, Iceland, Norway, and Sweden whose annual meetings are attended by cabinet members.

The introduction delineates the Scandinavian region, defines regionalism, and describes national attitudes toward it. Denmark and Finland have been the successive advocates of closer Nordic ties, meeting support from Sweden and opposition from Norway. Iceland is peripheral.

Chapter 2 traces the history of interparliamentary cooperation in Scandinavia, and establishes the continuity of the Nordic Council with predecessor organizations, which were also advisory bodies.

Chaper 3 dissects the organs of the Nordic Council. The national delegations have allowed power to be exercised by the five-man Presidium through the plural secretariat, for whom the committees are adjuncts.

Chapter 4 portrays the procedures followed at the annual sessions, from the introduction of matters to their final rejection or adoption as recommendations to the governments. The crystallization of unanimity at the lowest common denominator of agreement is seen to permeate committee deliberations and to reduce plenary sessions to routine acceptance of committee reports. The indicia of supranationality are enumerated and shown not to be present in the Nordic Council.

Chapter 5 describes the intergovernmental (as opposed to inter-parliamentary) organs of Scandinavian collaboration, and shows the failure of the Nordic Council to intrude itself into the bland fabric of executive or administrative cooperation, whether by direct or indirect means.

Chapter 6 supplies a chronology of the negotiations for a common Nordic market, which foundered first on Norwegian nationalism before being superseded by broader West European developments. As a case study in thwarted Scandinavian integration, these materials illustrate the conclusions drawn in preceding chapters.

The conclusion evaluates the Scandinavian experience in the light of the literature on regionalism. Homogeneity and heterogeneity are debunked as causal factors in integration. It is argued that union is initially voluntaristic, and that the inertia of national separatism cannot be overcome against the will of the least gregarious member of the region. Inter-Scandinavian relations are characterized by cooperation. Cooperation is defined, and the applicability of the Nordic variety to other regions is adumbrated.

In international relations, the countries of Scandinavia have found a "middle way" between anarchic use of force and political amalgamation. Among themselves, they will neither fight nor unite. Instead, they follow the way of cooperation, which requires persistent joint effort to increase mutual advantage. Moreover, "advantage" is officially defined—as exemplified in the 1962 Helsinki Agreement—to include the fostering of similarities and the elimination of hampering differences in legal system, social policy, transportation regulation, educational structure, and economic opportunity. Thus, the countries in question are practicing regionalism.

Because they retain their individuality and do not establish a superstate—whether unitary, federal, or supranational—the members of the region cannot be said to have integrated. Denmark, Finland, Iceland, Norway, and Sweden remain five separate countries with distinct foreign and domestic policies.

The process of regional accommodation is neither blameworthy nor exceptionally praiseworthy: it represents the pragmatic effort of real people to solve actual problems. Over time, these exertions have formed patterns. Their practical quality gives the recurrent themes of Scandinavian regionalism relevance to other parts of the world.

The momentum of each national bureaucratic apparatus in the Scandinavian countries makes regional coordination a formidable task. The Nordic Council has thrown the weight of its own miniscule civil service against the entrenched national administrations. The struggle has been an unequal one. Nor has public opinion been aroused to anything more than bland permissiveness. To the man on the street, Nordic problems lack palpable urgency.

Nonetheless, the postwar years have seen a steady accretion of concrete advances in regional harmonization. Scandinavia now comprises a passport union, a common employment market, and a reciprocal social security area. Uniform laws abound. And economic integration is taking place within the European Free Trade Association.

One development which has taken place since this book was written is worthy of mention. By the summer of 1967, Denmark, Norway, and Sweden had applied for membership in the European Community. To the extent that these applications must await the admission of Great Britain, the process of entering the common market will be lengthy and uncertain. It is not surprising that Finland is taking a wait-and-see stance. When the others have concluded negotiations, Finland will accommodate herself to them— always with a look over the shoulder for approval from the Soviet Union.

How this much came to pass, but no more and not sooner, is the burden of this book.

Santa Barbara, California

December, 1966

ACKNOWLEDGMENTS

THE AUTHOR is grateful for the Woodrow Wilson Foundation Traveling Fellowship in Political Science (1959–60) which provided a year's study in Scandinavia, and for the Honorary American-Scandinavian Foundation Fellowship which facilitated that study. The John Randolph Haynes and Dora Haynes Foundation kindly awarded a Faculty Summer Fellowship (1962), and the University of California supplied a Faculty Research Grant for the summer of 1966.

The Secretaries-General of the Nordic Council national delegations were very helpful. Staff members of the Nordic Council secretariats and of the parliamentary libraries in Copenhagen, Helsinki, Oslo, and Stockholm were also generous with their time, as were those of the Royal Library in Copenhagen and the National Library in Reykjavik.

The counsel of scholars from the Universities of Aarhus, Copenhagen, Gothenburg, Helsinki, Iceland, Lund, Oslo, and Stockholm was much appreciated. Professors Nils Andrén (Stockholm), Sven Henningsen (Copenhagen), and Nils Stjernquist (Lund) were especially encouraging. Professor Nils Herlitz (Stockholm) supplied information about the formative years of the Council; together with Hans Hedtoft, Herlitz was the father of the Nordic Council.

The author is indebted to cabinet members, members of Parliament, government officials, and private citizens who found time in their busy schedules to grant interviews.

Professor H. Peter Krosby of the University of Wisconsin and my colleagues Robert T. Anderson, Eric C. Bellquist, and Ernst B. Haas of the University of California (Berkeley) read the manuscript in one form or another and made criticisms and suggestions, a number of which were adopted. Research in Scandinavia was made enjoyable by the vast reservoir of good will built up by Professor Bellquist in years spent in Northern Europe as scholar and diplomat.

Finally, to Mary, Stella, Bob, Barbara, Andy, Robin, Scott, and Bruni, thanks for the pleasant distractions without which the task of writing might have become a drudge.

CONTENTS

One   INTRODUCTION
THE SCANDINAVIAN REGION   3

Two   INTERPARLIAMENTARY PREDECESSORS
OF THE NORDIC COUNCIL   15

Three   ORGANS OF THE NORDIC COUNCIL   26

Four   FROM PROPOSAL TO RECOMMENDATION—
PROCEDURE IN THE NORDIC COUNCIL   56

Five   THE NORDIC COUNCIL AND THE
GOVERNMENTS   110

Six   COMMON NORDIC MARKET NEGOTIATIONS   125

Seven   CONCLUSION   140

APPENDIX A: THE STATUTE OF THE
NORDIC COUNCIL, ANNOTATED   151

APPENDIX B: THE RULES OF PROCEDURE
OF THE NORDIC COUNCIL, ANNOTATED   157

APPENDIX C: THE DIRECTIONS FOR
COMMITTEE WORK, ANNOTATED   168

APPENDIX D: TREATY OF COOPERATION
BETWEEN DENMARK, FINLAND,
ICELAND, NORWAY, AND SWEDEN   174

APPENDIX E: THE STATUTE OF THE
NORDIC INTER-PARLIAMENTARY UNION   182

SELECTED BIBLIOGRAPHY   185

INDEX   191

CHARTS

1a. Organization of the Nordic Council during Annual Session   27

1b. Organization of the Nordic Council during the Interim   28

2. Number of Elected Members at Each Annual Session Who Have Attended a Previous Session, Either as an Elected Member (Including Promoted Alternates) or as a Ministerial Representative, 1954–62   30

3. Number of Party Chairmen or Floor Leaders, Presiding Officers of Parliament, or Former Cabinet Members Present as Elected Members at Each Annual Session, 1953–59   30

4. Ministerial Representatives in Attendance at Annual Sessions, 1953–62   32

5. Number of Terms on Same Standing Committee Previously Served by Standing Committee Members at the Seventh Annual Session of the Nordic Council, 1959   48

6. How a Proposal Becomes a Recommendation   57

7. Number of Items Offered for Consideration at Each Annual Session, 1953–62   61

8. Number of Recommendations on Which Memoranda Have Been Submitted by the Governments, 1954–61   66

9. Number of National Contributions to Memoranda, 1954–60   66

10. Participation in General Debate at Each Annual Session, 1953–62   76

11. Committee Proposals, 1953–62   83

12. Number of Matters Debated on Second Reading, 1953–62   86

13. Participation in Debate on Second Reading, 1953–62   87

14. Recommendations to the Governments, 1953–61   92

15. Negative Votes and Abstentions on Recommendations, 1953–61   93

THE NORDIC COUNCIL

A Study of Scandinavian Regionalism

Chapter One

INTRODUCTION:

THE SCANDINAVIAN REGION

Geographically, culturally, linguistically, and historically Scandinavia [1] is a region.

The Nordic countries, except for Iceland, are united geographically by the Baltic Sea. The heart of the area is the Scandinavian peninsula, whose north-and-south mountains divide Norway from Sweden for nearly a thousand miles. Apart from Norway's short northernmost boundary with the Soviet Union, Finland is the only country with which Sweden and Norway have a common land frontier. These three nations form a continuous land mass, partly severed by the Gulf of Bothnia, which separates southern Finland from Sweden. Scandinavia's only external land boundaries are with Germany and with Russia, which adjoins Finland to the east.

Denmark meets Germany in Schleswig, on the narrow and indefensible peninsula of Jutland. Zealand, Funen, and the smaller islands lie to the east of Jutland, and the entire country is half enveloped by the southern extremities of Norway and Sweden. The coast of Scania, Sweden's most southerly province, is visible from Copenhagen, located on the eastern edge of Zealand. One of the perennial proposals for Dano-Swedish cooperation is to build a bridge across or a tunnel under the Sound.

Iceland is also part of the geographical region of Scandinavia.

---

[1] Unless otherwise indicated, the term "Scandinavia" in any of its forms and the word "Nordic" include Denmark, Finland, Iceland, Norway, and Sweden. The political history of Scandinavia is sketched in the conclusion.

3

Her nearest neighbors are Greenland (to the west) and the Faeroes (to the southeast), each part of the Danish realm. The Faeroe Islands lie about halfway between Iceland and Norway. Iceland is remote, but less so from the other Nordic countries than from the rest of the world. The air age has pierced Icelandic isolation, however. Since World War II, Iceland's geographical relationships have been dominated by the fact that she lies on the great circle joining Moscow and New York City.

Sweden is the largest of the five countries (nearly 175,000 square miles), but Finland (130,000 square miles) and Norway (125,000 square miles) are also sizable. Iceland (40,000 square miles) is sparsely inhabited, especially in contrast to compact Denmark (16,500 square miles). Under the 1953 Constitution, Greenland's 840,000 square miles were made an integral part of the Danish kingdom, permitting the Danes to claim facetiously that they are the biggest nation in Western Europe. As a matter of fact, Finland, Norway, and Sweden are each comparable in area to France, Italy, West Germany, or the United Kingdom.

Scandinavia has a total population of over twenty million. Sweden (7,600,000 inhabitants) accounts for three eighths of this, and has twice as many people as Norway (3,700,000). Closer in size to Norway than to Sweden are Denmark (4,700,000) and Finland (4,600,000). More than distant location, Iceland's scanty population (190,000) prevents any expenditure of manpower in Nordic cooperation on a scale comparable to the others'.[2]

Danish, Norwegian, and Swedish are closely related languages. The native speaker of one of them may apprehend the others much as one would a distant dialect of his own. All three—or four, counting two versions of Norwegian—stem from Old Norse, though more remotely than does Icelandic. As is the case for the Faeroese, Icelanders must learn modern Scandinavian languages as foreign tongues, and usually study Danish in the public schools before they do English.

Finnish is completely different from the other languages of Scandinavia, or, for that matter, from any Indo-European language. It stems from Finno-Ugric stock, which the Finns share distantly with Hungarians. About 330,000 Finns speak Swedish as their native tongue, however, and others know it as a second language.

[2] Figures rounded from those supplied in *Yearbook of Nordic Statistics 1964* (Stockholm: Nordisk udredningsserie, No. 10, 1964), p. 8.

Lutheranism is uniformly established in Scandinavia. While there is freedom of religion, almost all of the people of the five Nordic countries are at least nominal members of the state-subsidized church.

Political similarities are also striking. In each country, members of Parliament are chosen by some system of proportional representation, and the cabinet is usually dependent on the continued support or toleration of the legislature. A government may stay in office until Parliament expresses its lack of confidence, or until the election period expires. In short, parliamentarism prevails. Each of the countries is organized on a unitary (nonfederal) basis, and has a prestigious central administration.

Denmark, Norway, and Sweden are constitutional monarchies whose royal families are closely related. Finland and Iceland are republics. Whether King or President, chiefs of state in Scandinavia are limited in authority, and political leadership is vested in the Prime Ministers and their cabinets. The President of Finland, however, is more than a figurehead and retains considerable autonomy in foreign affairs.

The Scandinavian states are characterized by multiparty systems. Most commonly, one finds a Social Democratic party, a Liberal party, an Agrarian party, a Conservative party, and a Communist party.[3] Indeed, these are the five parties represented in the Swedish Parliament. (The Bourgeois coalition holds a single additional independent mandate.) Elsewhere, neatness is blurred by schism.

The parties of the left get about half the vote in Scandinavian elections. In Denmark, Norway, and Sweden, the *Social Democrats* (called "Labor" in Norway, and "Social Democratic Labor" in Sweden) dominate the left, and have been able to form scant majority, strong minority, or dominant coalition governments for decades. This has permitted relatively stable cabinet government.

For all practical purposes, Sweden has had only two Prime Ministers in the last thirty years, both Social Democrats. Except for the summer of 1936, Per Albin Hansson was in office from 1932 until he died in 1946, at which time he was replaced by the present Prime Minister, Tage Erlander. Erlander headed a major-

[3] See Dankwart A. Rustow, "Scandinavia: Working Multiparty Systems," in Sigmund Neumann (ed.), *Modern Political Parties* (University of Chicago Press, 1956), pp. 169–93.

ity government from 1946 to 1951, a Social Democratic-Agrarian coalition from 1951 to 1957, and presently leads a Social Democratic Labor party minority cabinet.[4]

After thirty years in office, the Norwegian Labor party was replaced by a four-party coalition following the elections of September, 1965. An Agrarian, Per Borten, became Prime Minister in place of his Labor predecessor, Einar Gerhardsen. The coalition parties—Conservative, Center, Liberal, and Christian People— hold 80 of the Storting's 150 seats.

The Social Democrats are the largest party in Denmark and have headed the government most of the time since Prime Minister Thorvald Stauning formed a coalition with the Radical Liberals which lasted from 1929 until well into the Second World War. The Moderate Liberals supplied a cabinet from 1945 to 1947, and a Moderate Liberal–Conservative coalition was in office from 1950 to 1953. Even with Radical Liberal support, the Social Democratic coalition was one vote shy after the November, 1960, elections, and had to bring a nonpolitical member of Parliament from Greenland into the cabinet as Minister for Greenland Affairs, in order to secure a bare majority. This precarious margin was lost in the elections of September, 1964, whereupon the Social Democratic party formed a minority government. With some reshuffling, the minority government kept the reins of power after the elections of November, 1966.

Since resuming office in 1953, the Danish Social Democrats have been plagued by two untimely deaths and one premature retirement. Prime Minister Hans Hedtoft died in 1955, and his political heir, H. C. Hansen, passed away in 1960, both men in their early fifties. Hansen's successor, Viggo Kampmann, was forced to retire in 1962, due to poor health. He was replaced by Jens Otto Krag.

In Finland and Iceland, the Social Democrats have been reduced by splintering. The Icelandic party is the smallest of four represented in Parliament. President Asgeir Asgeirsson, now in his third four-year term as Iceland's chief of state, no longer indicates political affiliation; he was an active Social Democrat.

With fifty-five seats out of two hundred, the Finnish Social Democrats emerged as the largest party following the elections of

[4] See Nils Andrén, *Modern Swedish Government* (Stockholm: Hægström, 1961), pp. 219–25.

March, 1966. Prime Minister Rafael Paasio heads a "red-green" coalition of Social Democrats (including two factions), Communists, and Agrarians. From 1958 to 1961, and now again since 1966, the Social Democratic Opposition, renamed the Workers' and Peasants' Social Democratic Union, has been represented in the Finnish delegation to the Nordic Council in addition to the regular Social Democrats and Communists.

In Sweden, the *Liberal* party is second largest. The Swedish and Finnish groups call themselves "People's parties," while in Denmark and Norway they are known as "Left." In English, the Danish "Left" (*Venstre*) is often translated as "Moderate Liberal," in order to distinguish it from the Radical Liberals. The other Scandinavian Liberal parties recognize the Radical Liberals as their Danish counterpart. A third Danish liberal party, the Justice Union—based on Henry George's Single Tax principle —was eliminated from Parliament after the elections of November, 1960. Meanwhile, in 1965 a new group, the Liberal Center, splintered from the Moderate Liberals.

In Finland, the Freethinker's Union held a seat in Parliament from 1962 to 1966. Also, the Swedish People's party, discussed in the conclusion, contains liberal elements. Finally, one might consider the Christian People's party to be a second liberal party in Norway. There is no liberal party in Iceland, but the Conservative party there is based upon an earlier merger with liberals.

While concentrated in the Moderate Liberal fold, Danish farming interests are spread among several parties, and there is no exclusively *agrarian* group. Each of the other countries has a Farmer's party, called "Progressive" in Iceland and "Center" in Finland, Norway, and Sweden. Finland also has a Small Farmer's party. Until the March, 1966, elections, the Center (formerly "Agrarian Union") was the largest party in Finland. It has provided leadership in numerous governments. President Urho Kekkonen, elected in February, 1962, to a second six-year term, is an Agrarian.

Under various names, each Scandinavian country has a *Conservative* party. The Conservative party is the second largest in Norway. After World War II, the Danes expanded the designation of their traditional party to "Conservative People's party." A new radical conservative group, the Independent party, emerged in the November, 1960, elections, but was eliminated from Parliament in

1966. Finnish conservatives use the name of "National Coalition party," while Norwegian and Swedish groups carry the simple label "Right." The Independence party, to which Prime Minister Bjarni Benediktsson belongs, is the largest party in Iceland.

The *Communist* parties in Denmark, Norway, and Sweden are quite small. Only the Swedish party is represented in the national legislature. Danish Communists were eliminated in the elections of November, 1960. They were replaced by the Socialist People's party, which is Marxist and anti-NATO, but which claims independence from the Kremlin. Similarly, in Norway, a new Socialist People's party was created in 1961, splitting from Labor on the issue of disarmament and membership in NATO.[5] Communist parties are prominent in Finnish and Icelandic politics. In Finland, the People's Democratic League is the third largest of eight parties in Parliament.

The pattern of Scandinavian political parties has led Göran von Bonsdorff to conclude that "it is justifiable to speak of a special Nordic party system." [6] Not only do the Scandinavian countries share similar forms of government and parallel party systems, but the democratic parties of all the countries are united in basic philosophy. The Social Democrats have abandoned doctrinaire socialism, and the bourgeois parties have embraced broadened distribution of wealth. The result is a nearly universal commitment to full employment and social welfare.

From the foregoing, it is evident that the Scandinavian countries comprise an exclusive region, with Denmark, Norway, and Sweden as the core to which Finland and Iceland are firmly bound by culture, even if less so by location and language.

But what are the consequences of being a region? The Scandinavians have not always cooperated with one another, and not a few regions today are characterized by internecine strife. The very concept of a region implies that its component parts retain a separate identity and function at least partially as independent units.

"Regionalism" can be defined as officially sanctioned continuous effort to increase regional harmony by peaceful means. Similarities

[5] See James A. Storing, *Norwegian Democracy* (Boston: Houghton Mifflin, 1963), p. 143.

[6] Göran von Bonsdorff, "The Party Situation in Finland," in *Democracy in Finland* (Helsinki: Finnish Political Science Association, 1960), p. 18.

are heightened and differences lessened. This definition includes, but is broader than uses of the word "regionalism" which (legitimately) emphasize regional integration [7] or regional defense,[8] neither of which have characterized Scandinavian regionalism.

Forms of regionalism range from the highly unstructured to the rigidly institutionalized. The bulk of Scandinavian cooperative efforts are very informal. When collaboration is institutionalized, the vehicle of regionalism becomes an international organization. The Nordic Council is the primary regional organization for the harmonization of intra-Nordic policy.

Within a given region, the members may have quite divergent and shifting attitudes toward collaboration. Until supranationality is attained, or until the problem is superseded by union, the degree of multilateral implementation of regionalism is limited to that desired by the least regionally-minded member: "Measures resulting in integration evolve only . . . on the basis of the volition of the least cooperative among them." [9]

For over a century, until the present decade, the Danes were the most enthusiastic proponents of Scandinavian regionalism. When Bismarck established Prussian hegemony over an increasingly unified and belligerent Germany, Denmark needed help. She found comfort in the Pan-Scandinavian movement only until Sweden refused to come to her assistance in the disastrous war of 1864, at the conclusion of which Denmark was forced to cede Schleswig and Holstein to Prussia and Austria. The basic geopolitical need for support persisted, as demonstrated by the Nazi occupation of Denmark during World War II.

The search for Northern allies led the Danes to author almost every proposal for increased Scandinavian collaboration made in the last hundred years, including those which resulted in the formation of the Nordic Inter-Parliamentary Union in 1907, the inclu-

[7] Such as Ernst B. Haas, "The Challenge of Regionalism," *International Organization*, XII, No. 4 (1958), 440–58.

[8] Stephen S. Goodspeed, *The Nature and Function of International Organization* (New York: Oxford Press, 1959), stresses the security functions of regional organizations, and establishes (p. 549) that there "is no general agreement upon an exact definition of the term 'regionalism' for international organization."

[9] Ernst B. Haas and Peter H. Merkl, "Parliamentarians Against Ministers: The Case of Western European Union," *International Organization*, XIV, No. 1 (1960), 58.

sion of legislators in the 1949 Scandinavian Defense Alliance negotiations, the calling of joint meetings of the committees on citizenship of several parliaments in 1950, and the establishment of the Nordic Council in 1952.

Denmark alone gave highest priority to Scandinavian unity in the abortive Defense Alliance talks: the Swedes prized Scandinavian defense unity only if it did not entail extra-Scandinavian entanglements, the Norwegians only if it did.

The Danes still fear Germany, but the objective basis for apprehension has diminished with common Danish and German membership in the North Atlantic Treaty Organization. The alignments of the cold war and French-German *rapprochement* within Little Europe have eliminated the likelihood of war among Western European nations.

In recent years, then, Denmark has been able to follow economic advantage without compelling regard to the consequences for Nordic unity:

> Denmark's interest is indicated by the fact that she sells 28 per cent of her total exports to the EEC countries, 25 per cent to the United Kingdom, and 14 per cent to Sweden and Norway, while the three groups supply, respectively, 40, 18, and 15 per cent of her imports. A development which erects economic barriers between the EEC on the one hand and the United Kingdom and Scandinavia on the other is thus very unfortunate from a Danish point of view.
>
> When the British Government decided to seek admission to the EEC in the summer of 1961 Denmark, therefore, immediately made a similar decision.[10]

As early as 1960, the Danish government began to oppose further measures for Nordic integration, for fear that they might hinder admission into the European Economic Community. Denmark is no longer the most eager proponent of Scandinavian regionalism, and the generation of new forms of cooperation has devolved upon the Nordic Council itself, and upon Finland.

Finnish freedom of action in foreign affairs is circumscribed by the Paris Peace Treaty of 1947 and the Russo-Finnish Treaty of Friendship, Cooperation, and Mutual Assistance of 1948. The former provided for reparations to the Soviet Union, and limited the size and nature of Finland's armed forces, while the latter

[10] P. Nyboe Andersen, "Current Economic Problems," *Danish Foreign Office Journal*, No. 43 (1963), p. 22.

committed Finland to defend her own soil against attack by Germany or an ally of Germany, and to consult with the Soviet Union if such an attack should threaten. Both treaties obliged Finland and the Soviet Union "not to conclude any alliance or join any coalition directed against the other party."

By deciding which arrangements are directed against her, Russia has an effective veto over Finnish entrance into international organizations. The Kremlin initially considered the Nordic Council to be unfriendly, but relented in 1955.[11] The effectiveness of the Soviet veto is enhanced by Finland's partial economic dependence on the Eastern bloc, and by the pressure of domestic Communists and supporters, who control about one fourth of the seats in the Finnish Parliament.

The Finns are anxious to strengthen ties with the rest of Scandinavia for the same reason that the Danes sought support vis-à-vis Prussia: to make conquest costly. At the same time, the Paasikivi line (President J. K. Paasikivi, 1946–56), to which all Finnish political parties adhere, requires that Finland avoid even the appearance of evil, as far as arousing Russian suspicion is concerned. The other Scandinavian countries are very sympathetic to Finland in her delicate position.

Within the limits set by the Soviet Union, Scandinavian regionalism is a cardinal principle of Finnish foreign policy. The most important single function performed by the Nordic Council has been to foster this policy. Not only do Nordic ties bolster Finnish security directly, but they provide an entree into West European markets. Finland is particularly dependent upon foreign trade to dispose of the products of her forests, which represent over 70 per cent of the cash value of all Finnish exports. Her largest markets are in Britain, West Germany, Eastern Europe (representing about 15 per cent of Finland's total outside market), and the rest of Scandinavia.

When the negotiations for the creation of the European Free Trade Association were nearing fruition in the summer of 1959, only Finland—not a party to the talks—came forth with an official commitment to face the EFTA with the *fait accompli* of a pre-existing Nordic customs union. To Finland's great disappointment, Denmark, Norway, and Sweden had already agreed to enter EFTA

[11] See Klaus Törnudd, *Soviet Attitudes Towards Non-Military Regional Co-operation* (Helsinki: Centraltryckeriet, 1961), pp. 108–17.

on an individual basis and to forego a separate common Nordic market. With the formation of FINEFTA in 1961, Finland became an associate of EFTA. Should EFTA ever merge with EEC, both Finland and Sweden see Scandinavian regionalism as a force working against their exclusion, as neutrals, from the broadened common market.

Sweden has been consistently permissive in her attitude toward Scandinavian regionalism. Buffered from non-Nordic neighbors by the Baltic and by Finland, and with 150 years of successful neutrality, Sweden does not feel a need for alliances and does not seek them. Of all the Scandinavian countries, only Sweden was neither belligerent nor occupied during World War II. At the same time, as the largest country—whether measured by population, area, or industrial plant—Sweden does not fear domination by the three Scandinavian states which surround her. Moreover, her defense establishment—land, sea, and air—is substantial.

Perhaps to avoid accusations of regional imperialism, particularly from the Norwegians, the Swedes have, for the most part, let the other countries initiate proposals for new forms of Scandinavian cooperation. Sweden has then lent ready support to the others' proposals, even those which envisaged supranationality, while insisting only that they not jeopardize Swedish nonalignment in the cold war—a stance, Sweden argues, which helps Finland assuage the Soviet Union.

Norway, on the other hand, has consistently opposed Nordic integration. Following lonely defeat and Nazi occupation in the Second World War, the Norwegians were convinced by 1948 that they should not attempt neutrality in the East-West struggle. In 1948 and 1949, the Norwegians would accept a Scandinavian military alliance only within a framework of formal commitment to the West, a condition which Sweden could not accept.

"Norwegians cannot forget history, and there is not a single word which has a worse ring in Norwegian ears than Union," said the venerable Norwegian Conservative, C. J. Hambro.[12] Norwegian opposition to political integration stems from lingering resentment of past domination by her more populous Nordic neighbors. Few extremists would go so far as to oppose mere cooperation, but there is general apprehension of the possible loss of national free-

[12] C. J. Hambro, "Nordisk samarbeide eller Nordisk Råd," *Nordisk Kontakt,* No. 2 (1957), p. 2.

dom of action. Norway's acquiescence in Danish and Finnish proposals for new forms of Scandinavian collaboration has always
been contingent upon the removal of any provision in derogation
of national sovereignty.[13]

Norway is forced, as are Denmark and Sweden, to protect her
markets in Western Europe by participating in EFTA and by
seeking membership in EEC, if broadened to include Britain.
Norway's need for the EEC is somewhat less urgent than Denmark's. In 1962, 42 per cent of all Norwegian exports went to the
other EFTA countries (including 22 per cent to the other Scandinavian members of EFTA), while 27 per cent went to the common
market. On the import side, Norway received 37 per cent of total
imports in 1962 from the EFTA bloc (again including 22 per cent
from the other Nordic EFTA nations), and 30 per cent from the
EEC. Norway has proportionally more intra-Scandinavian trade
than any of the other Nordic countries.[14] On the Nordic scene,
however, the Norwegians see little opportunity for further penetration of complementary neighboring economies with timber or fish,
and some are concerned that the more advanced and efficient
industrial development of Denmark and Sweden, especially the
latter, might stifle Norwegian growth and reduce the Norwegian
economy to colonial subservience.

To all these concerns, Iceland has been a bystander, and not a
participant. Other issues of foreign policy have far overshadowed
Nordic ones. In the postwar period, Icelanders have had to recon-
cile themselves to the continued presence of American troops on
Icelandic soil, as part of Iceland's NATO commitment.[15] New
markets, mostly in Eastern Europe, have been found for the fish
which are Iceland's sole export crop. Finally, the dispute with
Britain over the breadth of Icelandic territorial waters was re-

[13] Article 93 was added to the Norwegian Constitution in 1962, authorizing
transfer of national authority to supranational organizations. This innovation
was in response to the impetus of West European integration, and culminated
after proposals for a common Nordic market had been abandoned. See
Stanley V. Anderson, "Supranational Delegation Clauses in Scandinavian
Constitutions," *Western Political Quarterly,* XVIII, No. 4 (December, 1965),
840–47.

[14] See Knut Getz Wold, "Norge, Norden or markedsproblemene," *Nordisk
Kontakt,* No. 10 (1963), pp. 581–82.

[15] See Donald E. Nuechterlein, *Iceland: Reluctant Ally* (Ithaca, N.Y.:
Cornell University Press, 1961).

solved.[16] The Icelandic Prime Minister attempted, without success, to get the Nordic Council to support claims against Britain at the second annual session in 1954.

Whenever frustrated in matters of political, economic, or military collaboration, the Scandinavian countries have turned to cultural and social cooperation. These latter, together with the question of improved communications, have been the only topics of Nordic cooperation which have directly concerned Iceland.

While enthusiasm for Scandinavian regionalism varies among the nations and over time, there remains as a common residue "an active desire to preserve and promote . . . regional identity." [17]

We have now characterized the Scandinavian region and described prevailing policies toward it. Indifference, opposition, enthusiasm, support: these are the national postures whose tensions shaped the organs of Scandinavian regionalism.

[16] See Morris Davis, *Iceland Extends Its Fisheries Limits* (Norway: Scandinavian University Books, 1963).

[17] Vincent H. Malmström, *Norden: Crossroads of Destiny and Progress* (Princeton, N.J.: Van Nostrand, 1965), p. 5.

Chapter Two

INTERPARLIAMENTARY
PREDECESSORS
OF THE NORDIC COUNCIL

As an interparliamentary body, the Nordic Council is distinguished by the fact that cabinet members attend both plenary sessions and committee meetings. In the latter, the frank exchange between ministers and members of Parliament has made the Council a truly deliberative body.

While the combination was new, each basic aspect of Nordic Council organization had been used by a predecessor organ:

1. Regular meetings of Scandinavian members of Parliament commenced with the Nordic Inter-Parliamentary Union (NIPU) in 1907.

2. Cabinet members sometimes attended the NIPU sessions, but the impetus for regular ministerial participation in meetings with legislators came from the 1949 Scandinavian Defense Alliance conferences.

3. At the committee level, joint meetings of Scandinavian lawmakers commenced into 1950, in the course of enactment of a new uniform citizenship law, and was continued by the Nordic Parliamentary Committee for Traffic Freedom, founded in 1951. Cabinet members joined in the 1950 citizenship law hearings.

THE NORDIC INTER-PARLIAMENTARY UNION

The first regular meetings of Scandinavian members of Parliament took place within the larger context of the Inter-

Parliamentary Union, founded in 1889. On Danish initiative, the Nordic Inter-Parliamentary Union constituted itself in 1907 as a regional unit of the universal organization; Finland and Iceland joined after World War I.[1] Except as interrupted by war, meetings of delegates of the NIPU took place annually in the several capitals from 1907 to 1947, and then every other year until 1957, when the final meeting was held.

Most Scandinavian legislators, except for a score or more Norwegians, derive membership in the Nordic Inter-parliamentary Union from their participation in the parent union. About fifteen from each Parliament, though fewer from Iceland, used to attend the two-day NIPU meetings as official delegates of their national groups. Others, including occasional cabinet members, came as special invitees.

Four members from each national group, including the group chairman and vice-chairman, composed an executive board. The chairman of the host group of the most recent meeting of delegates was automatically President of the NIPU.

There are many institutional similarities between the Council and the NIPU. These can be capsulized as expressions of the principle of national equality—with some exceptions for Finland and Iceland—in use of language and in the selection of members, officers, and staff: Danish, Norwegian, and Swedish are used interchangeably; offices are rotated or distributed evenly; secretariats are plural.

The Nordic Council differs from the Nordic Inter-Parliamentary Union in the following ways: the Council is characterized by greater procedural formality; the annual sessions of the Council last longer than did those of the NIPU, and many more matters are taken up for consideration; the Council pays greater attention to publicity and public relations; the annual sessions of the Council have civil servants and experts in attendance, as well as regular sizable ministerial delegations; finally, the Nordic Council has created a permanent bureaucracy and has undertaken considerable interim activity.

The proposal for an official permanent organ of Scandinavian interparliamentary consultation, from which the Nordic Council emerged, was made at the twenty-eighth meeting of delegates of the Nordic Inter-Parliamentary Union, held in Stockholm in Au-

[1] The Statute of the NIPU is found in Appendix E.

gust, 1951. The annual sessions of the Nordic Council have since made the NIPU superfluous, although the national groups continue to function in the original Inter-Parliamentary Union.

SCANDINAVIAN DEFENSE ALLIANCE NEGOTIATIONS

On the initiative of the Danish Foreign Minister, parliamentarians participated in the 1949 Scandinavian Defense Alliance conferences in Copenhagen and Oslo. The Danish, Norwegian, and Swedish Prime Ministers, Foreign Ministers, and Ministers of Defense were joined by twenty-four leading members of Parliament, eight from each country, representing all of the democratic parties. Civil servants were also present, supplemented in Oslo by key diplomatic personnel.

The conferences included plenary meetings at which the delegates were seated alphabetically rather than by country, meetings of the national delegations, and meetings of the nine ministers. At the five-hour plenary session on the opening day of the Copenhagen conference (January 22–24, 1949), all nine ministers took the floor, followed by nine prominent parliamentary representatives. The legislators reiterated the positions taken by their respective governments.

The negotiations were not successful: Denmark (and later Iceland) followed Norway into NATO, while Sweden (like Finland) remained outside any bloc. The procedures were successful, however, and the official communiqué from the Oslo conference of January 29–30, 1949, noted the following: "[This is] the first time that parliamentary representatives have participated together with Cabinet Members in negotiations of this kind. This form of conference has shown itself to be of great value in the illumination and clarification of the views which prevail in each country."

When proposals for military integration were replaced by proposals for economic integration, as discussed in Chapter 6, similar techniques of parliamentary participation were adopted. On four occasions (apart from annual sessions) from 1955 to 1959, elected members to the Nordic Council joined in governmental deliberations on the proposed common Nordic market.

The first of these two-day conferences was held in October, 1955. Ten cabinet members were present, four from Denmark and three each from Norway and Sweden, including the Prime Ministers and the Ministers of Economic Cooperation. The Council was represented by the Presidium, the chairman and vice-chairman of the Standing Committee on Economic Matters, and the Secretaries-General. All of the ministerial representatives were Social Democrats. The Danish and Swedish parliamentarians included three representatives of the bourgeois parties, but the sole member of Parliament from Norway was a Laborite. Thus, the large minority in the Norwegian Parliament which opposed a common Nordic market was unrepresented.

In addition to the question of economic cooperation, the conference considered matters of Council procedures and relations with the governments and made arrangements for Finnish accession to the Council. Some of the Council's representatives and staff had hoped that, at the least, agreement to form a common Nordic market could be reached. They did not express publicly their disappointment that such was not the case, but the opportunity for Scandinavian economic integration to keep pace with developments in the rest of Europe was rapidly disappearing.

Subsequent Council-government conferences dealt with the relationship between the proposed common Nordic market and other imminent European free trade areas. On three occasions—in November, 1957, September, 1958, and August, 1959—the Nordic Council's Standing Committee on Economic Matters, expanded to include representatives of those parties in the Council not already included in the committee, met with the Presidium of the Council and the Ministers of Economic Cooperation.

Similarly, one elected member for each of the nonrepresented parties was invited to attend the pertinent hearings of the Standing Committee on Economic Matters at the annual sessions of the Nordic Council in 1958 and 1959. Thirteen ministerial representatives attended the November, 1958, sessional hearings. In November, 1959, by which time the question had become moot, only the Ministers of Cooperation from Denmark, Norway, and Sweden attended the sessional committee hearings on economic cooperation.

Two years later, at the instigation of the Presidium, the expanded Standing Committee on Economic Matters met with the Economic Cooperation Ministers from the four larger countries on August 19–20, 1961, to discuss the Nordic implications of British application for membership in the European Economic Community.

Altogether, then, there have been a half-dozen free trade area conferences at which almost all of the parties in the Nordic Council were represented. At only one, however, was ministerial participation on a par with that of the 1949 Defense Alliance negotiations.

The striking difference between the Defense Alliance and the common market negotiations, insofar as parliamentary participation is concerned, is that in the former, the decision not to enter into an alliance was made in connection with conferences in which the legislators participated, while in the latter, the decision not to create a common Nordic market as part of the larger European Free Trade Association was made without the knowledge of the legislators, who were simply faced with a *fait accompli* at the meeting of the expanded Standing Committee on Economic Matters in August, 1959.

It is clear from the common market conferences that the Nordic Council is the parliamentary participant in negotiations which consider basic changes in intra-Nordic relationships. It is equally clear that such negotiations must be infrequent. Perhaps the Council's readiness for such deliberations is in itself adequate justification for its existence. In any event, the felicity of joint ministerial and parliamentary deliberations in the Defense Alliance negotiations was important in securing their continuation in common market deliberations and at the annual sessions of the Nordic Council.

More recently, the Council has sponsored a series of informational conferences focused on a single salient subject matter. The first of these was held in Copenhagen on April 13 to 15, 1964, and treated with plans for bridging the Sound between Denmark and Sweden.[2] A year later, a conference on scientific research was held in Helsinki. Again in Copenhagen, a meeting on the harmonization of taxation in Scandinavia took place on April 25 and 26, 1966. These conferences are attended by elected members to the Nordic Council and other specially interested legislators, by cabinet members, civil servants, scientists, and representatives of business and professional groups.

UNIFORM CITIZENSHIP LAW DELIBERATIONS

Another innovation in Scandinavian parliamentary cooperation occurred in May, 1950, when a joint meeting of members of the

[2] See *Nordiska rådets öresundskonferens den 13–15 april 1964* (Stockholm: Nordisk udredningsserie, No. 5, 1964), 155 pp.

appropriate committees of the parliaments of Denmark, Norway, and Sweden was held in the course of enactment of a new uniform citizenship law.

In August, 1949, after three years of deliberations, a committee of experts had submitted a report with a proposal for a new law on citizenship, essentially the work of the committee's Swedish secretariat. Proposals were introduced into the legislatures of the three countries, and differences arose as they progressed through the Danish and Swedish parliaments.

Again on Danish initiative, a conference was held in Copenhagen on May 8–9, 1950. The Danish Minister of the Interior and the Norwegian and Swedish Ministers of Justice attended, together with seventeen legislators from Denmark, Norway, and Sweden. Plenary meetings alternated with caucuses of the national delegations. In the plenary sessions, the delegations were seated as units, with the respective committee chairmen and cabinet members in the first row. The result of the conference was greater, but not complete, uniformity: agreement was reached on the issue of married women's nationality, but not on that of traitors' expatriation.

The Nordic Council has not been able to coordinate terminal deliberations on proposed uniform legislation. The parliamentary committees are reluctant to delegate their responsibilities to outsiders, and membership is too small to promise any appreciable overlap between Council committee and parliamentary committee. Nor can the Council-in-session be expected to meet at a time propitious for final negotiations on uniformity.

In a manner similar to that seen in the 1950 uniform citizenship law deliberations, representatives of the parliamentary committees considering governmental proposals on uniform copyright legislation met jointly in Stockholm for two days in June, 1960. The Nordic Council was ignored, in spite of the fact that it met in annual session six weeks later. (The convenience of this coincidence was dissipated by the fact that the session was held in Iceland.)

Nevertheless, the effectiveness of the joint labors in 1950 was an inspiration to the founders of the Nordic Council as an illustration of the practicability of interparliamentary cooperation on concrete measures of moderate importance. The participation of cabinet members in these hearings provided a precedent which has been adopted by the Nordic Council in its sessional committee work.

THE NORDIC PARLIAMENTARY COMMITTEE
FOR TRAFFIC FREEDOM

On January 19, 1951, the Swedish Social Democrat, Rolf Edberg, introduced a motion in the Swedish Parliament urging the
creation of an interparliamentary committee for the facilitation of
travel among the Scandinavian peoples. He was joined in the
motion by the floor leaders of the major political parties. The
Standing Committee on Foreign Affairs presented a unanimously
favorable report on the motion, which was accepted without dissent on April 11, 1951.

On January 24, 1951, five days after the initial motion in the
Swedish Parliament, Hans Hedtoft, the leader of the Danish Social
Democrats, solicited the Liberal-Conservative coalition government's views on the same matter during the question period in
Parliament. Foreign Minister Ole Bjørn Kraft indicated that the
government was favorably disposed to the creation of such an
interparliamentary commission and would be willing to take the
matter up with the several party spokesmen.

Meanwhile, in Norway, the Norwegian group of the Nordic
Inter-Parliamentary Union made a similar proposal to the Presidium of the Norwegian Parliament. (Easing of travel restrictions
had been on the agenda of the twenty-seventh meeting of delegates
of the NIPU, in 1949.) The Presidium transmitted the proposal to
the Foreign Office, which approved it, on condition that Norway's
slender foreign exchange reserves be protected. On April 26, 1951,
the Presidium—with the exception of the Conservative, C. J.
Hambro—recommended to Parliament that Norway participate in
the project.

Finnish and Icelandic participation was arranged by the five
governments later in 1951. Denmark, Norway, and Sweden each
chose five members of Parliament to serve on the committee, while
Finland appointed a six-man group, of whom three were members
of Parliament. Iceland did not follow suit, but later sent one or two
observers—members of Parliament or government officials—to a
few of the meetings.

Each national group chose a chairman, and the chairmen constituted a Presidium. Initial studies were carried out by the Presidium, which met alternatively in Denmark, Finland, Norway, and
Sweden. The Presidium was assisted by staff and by consultants,

who also held meetings. Preliminary reports were submitted to the separate national groups and then presented at plenary meetings of the committee for final consideration.

On the average, two plenary meetings were held each year from 1951 until 1956. With the removal of many minor impediments to travel and with the elimination of the requirement of passports for fellow Scandinavians, the Parliamentary Committee for Traffic Freedom felt that its work was done and that it should be replaced by a smaller permanent committee. The Nordic Council accepted a final report and suggested in Recommendation 1/1957 that the governments establish a new permanent organ composed of two members of Parliament from Denmark, Finland, Norway, and Sweden, and one from Iceland.

The governments responded by setting up the Nordic Traffic Committee, with the membership suggested by the Council and staffed by a civil servant from each country. Thus, after several years of coexistence with the Council, and after completing its major tasks, the Parliamentary Committee for Traffic was merged into the Nordic Council as a de facto interim committee.

The Nordic Council has attempted to take over the work methods of the Nordic Parliamentary Committee for Traffic Freedom, which had been established specifically to overcome bureaucratic inertia: the Nordic Council also attempts to act as a pressure group vis-à-vis the administration. It must be noted, however, that an energetic consensus was reached at a positive and concrete level in the Nordic Parliamentary Committee for Traffic Freedom. In the Council, consensus has often crystallized at a level less demanding of change.

APPRAISAL

It is easy to enumerate important advances in postwar Scandinavian cooperation—such as the passport union, the common labor market, and reciprocal extension of social security—but it is difficult to assess the credit which should be given to the individual organs.[3]

Thus, the Nordic Parliamentary Committee for Traffic Freedom secured the elimination of passports for Scandinavians within Scan-

[3] Frantz Wendt, *The Nordic Council and Co-operation in Scandinavia* (Copenhagen: Munksgaard, 1959), conveniently divides his categories of cooperation into pre-Council and post-Council periods.

dinavia, while the establishment of a full-fledged passport union occurred under the aegis of the Nordic Council. The Convention on Social Security for Nordic Citizens Residing in Neighboring Nordic Countries came into effect on July 2, 1954; thereafter, the Council worked for the consolidation of sixteen outstanding agreements, and a new comprehensive convention became operative on November 1, 1956. Similarly, the Convention on Labor Exchange was drafted before the Council came into existence, but the Nordic Council has been working for its expansion, particularly as regards medical personnel. Credit for harmonizing internal legislation must be shared with the private Meetings of Nordic Jurists, which date back to 1872.

The over-all picture is clearly one of great continuity with predecessor organs. In addition to the carry-over just described, the Nordic Council borrows many details of parliamentary procedure from the several parliaments.

The mere tracing of origins does not explain the existence of the Council. The convergence of antecedents would not have occurred if it had not been for the initiative taken by Hans Hedtoft. Hedtoft was Danish Prime Minister during the Defense Alliance negotiations in 1948 and 1949. He led the Danes in their futile efforts to establish a common Nordic position in the cold war. In 1951, after his Social Democratic government had been unseated, Hans Hedtoft posed the question in Parliament which led to Danish participation in the Nordic Parliamentary Committee for Traffic Freedom, and served as first chairman of the Danish group in the committee.

Later in 1951, Hedtoft suggested the creation of the Nordic Council at the August meeting of delegates of the Nordic Inter-Parliamentary Union,[4] and served on the five-man drafting team which prepared a Statute for the Council. (The initial draft was written by the Swedish Conservative, Nils Herlitz.) As chairman of the first Danish national delegation, Hedtoft was a charter member of the Presidium of the Nordic Council, and the first President of the Council, in which capacity he issued the summons to the initial session, which was held in February, 1953.

[4] As chairman of the Danish delegation, Hans Hedtoft was giving expression to the resolution adopted by the delegation in May, 1951, following the motion of the Radical Liberal Bertel Dahlgaard. See Bertel Dahlgaard, *Kamp og Samarbejde* (Gentofte, Denmark: Fremad, 1964), p. 155.

What kind of a Council did Hedtoft want? At the 1951 meeting of delegates of the NIPU, he urged the creation of an interparliamentary body which would meet for a week once or twice a year, to make recommendations to the governments. The proposed Statute which emerged from the drafting committee provided for voting participation in Council deliberations by the Prime Ministers and Foreign Ministers of the member nations. As a consequence of cabinet solidarity and cabinet dependence on the continued confidence or toleration of a majority in Parliament, this would have given the Council effective authority in matters on which the cabinet members voted. Having taken a stand in the Council, the governments would normally take the same stand at home. (If this provision had been retained, though, the voting ministers would probably have abstained in most cases.)

At the request of the Norwegians, the provision for ministerial voting was deleted at the March, 1952, meetings of the Foreign Ministers of Denmark, Norway, and Sweden and the Icelandic envoy in Denmark. The other representatives also acceded to Norwegian insistence that the Council secretariat be kept small and that the Statute be adopted by parallel enactment rather than by binding treaty.[5]

In spite of these concessions, the formation of the Council was generally opposed by the bourgeois parties in Norway and by some Agrarians and Conservatives in Iceland. The Nordic Council came into existence with the adoption of the Statute by the parliaments of Denmark, Norway, and Sweden in May and June of 1952. Only the Danes enacted the Statute as a law and promulgated it as a treaty. The others used parliamentary resolutions. Iceland became a charter member by adoption of the Statute in December, 1952. As part of a relaxation of relations between Finland and the Soviet Union, Finland was able to join late in 1955.

Hans Hedtoft viewed the prime ministership which he resumed in 1953 in part as an opportunity to make Nordic cooperation a more vital part of Scandinavian political life. Without consulting Foreign Minister H. C. Hansen, he placed Nordic Council affairs in the Prime Minister's portfolio. Hedtoft died in 1955, while attending the third annual session of the Nordic Council in Stockholm.

One can only speculate as to the effect which continued applica-

[5] See Stanley V. Anderson, "Negotiations for the Nordic Council," *Nordisk Tidsskrift for International Ret,* XXXIII, No. 1–2 (1963), 23–33.

tion of Hedtoftian vigor and persuasiveness might have had on Nordic intergovernmental relations, particularly during the crucial common market negotiations in 1958 and 1959. Perhaps there would have been no substantial difference. In any event, the Scandinavian countries have not united militarily or politically, and economic integration has occurred only as a consequence of the formation of the European Free Trade Association, of which Denmark, Norway, and Sweden are members, and Finland an associate.

Having refused to entertain supranationality, the Scandinavians use the Nordic Council, together with other official organs of cooperation, as an intergovernmental substitute for the authoritative regional decision-making bodies that might have been. How these substitutes work will be described in the succeeding chapters.

Chapter Three

ORGANS OF THE NORDIC COUNCIL

The Nordic Council is composed of national delegations elected by and from the five parliaments. The Icelandic delegation has five members, while each of the others has sixteen. Alternates are designated to replace absent or prematurely retiring members. During the annual sessions of the Council, the sixty-nine elected members are augmented by cabinet members as designated by the governments. Only the elected members may vote.

The Council sets up five standing committees. Each national delegation appoints a working committee. Together, the working committees comprise a Joint Working Committee.

The chairman of the delegation leads the national working committee, and serves on the five-man Presidium of the Nordic Council. There are five national secretariats, each headed by a Secretary-General. The Secretary-General to the host delegation functions as Chief Clerk to the Council-in-session, while members of the Presidium alternate as Speaker (see charts 1a and 1b).

THE NATIONAL DELEGATIONS

In choosing elected members to the Nordic Council, each Parliament uses a form of proportional representation. A mathematical formula is applied to allocate the seats among the parties. By mutual agreement, there have been occasional deviations from the formula. When the allocation is made, each party decides which of its members shall be chosen, and the result is ratified by the legislature. Consequently the Council is a microcosm of the parent

CHART 1a.

ORGANIZATION OF THE NORDIC COUNCIL DURING ANNUAL SESSION

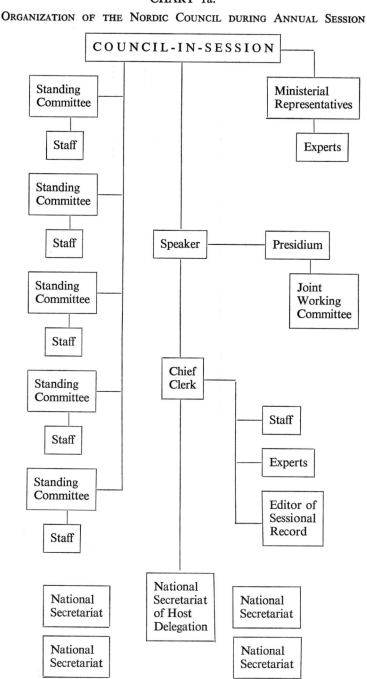

CHART 1b.

ORGANIZATION OF THE NORDIC COUNCIL DURING THE INTERIM

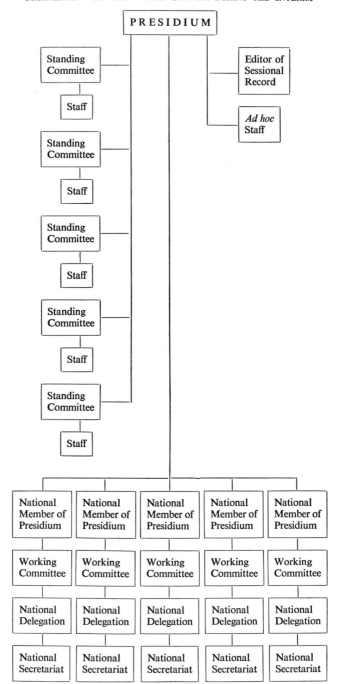

bodies. The Social Democratic parties have slightly less than half of the elected members' seats in the Council. Liberals, conservatives, and agrarians follow in that order, closer in size to one another than to the Social Democrats. Together, these four groups have 90 per cent of the seats. The remaining places are divided among the communist parties of Denmark, Finland, and Iceland, the Swedish People's party of Finland, and the Christian People's party of Norway.[1]

Three or four representatives of the Finnish People's Democratic League have been included in all Finnish delegations. The communists have been too few in Denmark, Norway, and Sweden to obtain representation in the Nordic Council, with the exception of the Danish Socialist People's party, whose founder, Aksel Larsen, defected from the Danish Communist party after Soviet suppression of the 1956 Hungarian uprising. Larsen has been attending annual sessions since 1961.

Even though the Icelandic Labor Alliance has one more seat in Parliament than the Social Democrats, the latter have always been represented in the Nordic Council, while the former sent an elected member only for the years 1957 to 1963, during part of which time (1956 to 1958) the communist Alliance participated in a coalition government with the Agrarians and the Social Democrats.

Members are elected for annual terms preceding each annual session. Deputy delegates are elected at the same time and in number equal to the elected members. The elected membership of the Council has been characterized by great continuity (see chart 2).

Initially, Finland had more turnover than the others, an indication that the Council was being used there somewhat more for general orientation than for the development of specialized competence. The Norwegian delegation has also used the annual sessions partly for acclimatization. Thus, the Presidium, speaking through the Swedish secretariat, noted that:

In the Labor Party in Norway there have been occasional changes in the party's group in the Council with the idea of letting more Members of Parliament participate in the Council's meetings to

[1] For detailed analysis of attendance at the annual sessions by elected members and ministerial representatives, with charts keyed in English and Danish, see Stanley V. Anderson, "Medlemmerne i Nordisk Råd, 1953–1959," *Statsvetenskaplig Tidskrift*, LXV, No. 2–3 (1962), 174–92.

CHART 2.

NUMBER OF ELECTED MEMBERS AT EACH ANNUAL SESSION WHO HAVE ATTENDED A PREVIOUS SESSION, EITHER AS AN ELECTED MEMBER (INCLUDING PROMOTED ALTERNATES) OR AS A MINISTERIAL REPRESENTATIVE, 1954–62

	Annual session in:								
	1954	1955	1956	1957	1958	1959	1960	1961	1962
Denmark	9	15	15	14	12	13	14	15	15
Finland	x	x	x	12	10	12	12	13	10
Iceland	3	2	4	4	5	4	4	5	5
Norway	8	14	16	14	14	16	15	15	14
Sweden	13	13	13	14	15	15	15	13	14
Total	33	44	48	58	56	60	60	61	58

x = Finland not yet a member.

make them familiar with the work of the Council. . . . In the Swedish Delegation so far, continuity has been felt to be more valuable, and no change of members for the above reason has taken place.[2]

On the other hand, Sweden has more frequently permitted alternate delegates to substitute temporarily for a full elected member, usually in order to permit the alternate to advocate a particular measure before the Council.

At each session, approximately one half of the elected members have been key politicians at home (see chart 3). When the pres-

CHART 3.

NUMBER OF PARTY CHAIRMEN OR FLOOR LEADERS, PRESIDING OFFICERS OF PARLIAMENT, OR FORMER CABINET MEMBERS PRESENT AS ELECTED MEMBERS AT EACH ANNUAL SESSION, 1953–59

	Annual session in:							
	1953	1954	1955	1956	1957	1958	1959	Total
Denmark	11	10	9	8	9	10	8	65
Finland	x	x	x	13	8	7	7	35
Iceland	3	4	4	3	5	5	3	27
Norway	9	7	5	6	6	8	8	49
Sweden	5	8	9	8	10	10	10	60
Total	28	29	27	38	38	40	36	

x = Finland not yet a member.

[2] *Nordisk Råd: 6. sesjon, 1958* ("The Nordic Council: Sixth Session, 1958," hereinafter cited as *1958 Record;* the other annual records will be similarly cited), p. 1626.

ence of the ministerial representatives is added to that of the prominent elected members, the result is a potential constitutional convention. This power, even though unused, makes each annual session a dramatic event.

In a sense, the ministerial representatives are part of the national delegations during the annual sessions. Originally, it was thought that the ministerial representatives to the Nordic Council would also be part of their respective national delegations during the period between sessions. Thus, the Swedish Prime Minister led the first two meetings of the Swedish national delegation in 1952, until the delegation elected a chairman. With this single exception, however, the expectations have not materialized, and only the regulations for the Swedish Nordic Council delegation retain vestiges of the notion of continuous governmental membership: Swedish ministerial representatives are included formally as nonvoting members of the national delegation.

Immediately after the first annual session, the draftsman of the Statute and chairman of the Swedish delegation, Nils Herlitz, recognized that "It would be difficult to distinguish between those [Ministers] who had been appointed to the most recent Session and the others. . . ." [3] A 1959 report to the Swedish Parliament summed up the procedure for ministerial appointment in that country as follows:

> . . . [A]ccording to previous practice, the Government appoints its representatives just for the relatively short period during which a Session is taking place [and the] Ministerial Representatives have not come to participate in the Delegation's work except during Sessions. However, during the period between Sessions, Cabinet Members have participated in the Delegation's deliberations on various matters by special invitation. [4]

The governments send sizable and influential ministerial delegations to the sessions (see chart 4). As a consequence of the political complexion of the various governments, the Social Democrats send about five-eighths of all ministerial representatives, while the Agrarians, Liberals, and Conservatives follow in that order.

[3] Minutes of the meeting of the Joint Working Committee, February 22, 1953, p. 6.

[4] *Bankoutskottets utlåtande* (Report of the Swedish Riksdag's Joint Committee on Banking), 37/1959, p. 14.

CHART 4.

MINISTERIAL REPRESENTATIVES IN ATTENDANCE AT ANNUAL SESSIONS,
1953–62

Annual session in:

	1953	1954	1955	1956	1957	1958	1959	1960	1961	1962
Denmark	5 *	7	4	10 *	8	7	6	6	14 *	10
Finland	x	x	x	5	10 *	6	5	5	6	9*
Iceland	1	2	0	1	0	0	0	7 *	2	1
Norway	4	10 *	6	8	8	8 *	8	4	6	6
Sweden	5	5	10 *	5	7	6	11 *	5	10	9
Total	15	24	20	29	33	27	30	27	38	35

* Host country.
x = Finland not yet a member.

The Prime Ministers of Denmark, Finland (since 1956), Norway, and Sweden have attended nearly all the sessions; Foreign Ministers and Ministers of Justice are also regular participants, while the holders of other portfolios come more sporadically. After a prolonged lapse, Icelandic ministerial attendance was reestablished in 1960.

The Council has profited from the presence of the cabinet members at the annual sessions:

> In the Council of Europe, the Assembly, acting on its own, has adopted recommendations which in some cases have been considered unrealistic or impractical by the Committee of Ministers. . . .
> In the Nordic Council, on the other hand, the presence of Ministers in the Assembly and committees has probably made for more realistic recommendations than has been the case in the Council of Europe. Ministers have been able to point out whether a proposal is feasible and to indicate the possible practical difficulties.[5]

All of the Nordic Council national delegations except the Icelandic submit annual reports to the home parliaments, describing their participation in the most recent annual session. The reports are skeletal—especially the Finnish and Norwegian ones—and are accepted perfunctorily. The Council's recommendations are appended to the reports, but are not considered on their merits. The parliaments wait instead for the governments to introduce legisla-

[5] Einar Løchen, "A Comparative Study of Certain European Parliamentary Assemblies," L'Annuaire Européen/The European Yearbook, IV (1958), 156.

tion on matters of Scandinavian cooperation. On those occasions when the reports of the national delegations have given rise to discussion, the topic for debate has almost always been the Nordic Council itself and Nordic cooperation in general, rather than any specific proposal.

The specific duties of the delegations may be summarized as follows:

1. to choose a Secretary-General and staff;
2. to nominate members for committees set up by the Council during sessions;
3. to appoint members to new interim committees;
4. to replace members retiring from the Presidium or from Council committees during the interim; and,
5. to submit an annual report to the home Parliament on Nordic Council activities.

While the views of the members may be solicited individually, the national delegations seldom meet as a body between sessions, but come to life only at the annual sessions. During the sessions, the delegations meet separately almost daily. These are business affairs, as contrasted with the luncheon and evening gatherings of those who bear the same party label, which are social events.

THE WORKING COMMITTEES

The working committees are not mentioned in the Statute of the Nordic Council. Section 25 of the Rules of Procedure directs each delegation to "elect a working committee to consult with the Presidium and with the other working committees on questions concerning the organization of the Council's activities." Section 16 of the Rules establishes the working committees as nominating bodies.

There is no reference to the working committees in the enabling legislation for the Nordic Council in Denmark, Iceland, or Norway. Statutory recognition of the Finnish working committee is of fairly recent origin, and reflects current efforts to make Scandinavian cooperation a vital part of domestic political life. As for Sweden, detailed regulation of the working committee is consonant with the comprehensive circumscription of parliamentary organs which is characteristic there, and contrasts with the greater informality of political organization in Denmark—which in turn tends to explain the Danish failure to surround its working committee with formal rules. Norway has resisted all efforts to intrude the Nordic Council into the constitutional fabric of Norwegian government; the basic enactment of the Statute of the Nordic Council has never been amplified.

The Finnish law on the Nordic Council delegation authorizes the working committee to carry out the day-to-day activities of the delegation, and to engage personnel other than the Secretary-General.[6]

Paragraph 4 of the parliamentary regulations governing the Swedish Nordic Council delegation gives the following directions:

> The Working Committee shall consist of the Chairman and Vice-Chairman of the Delegation and three other members. The former shall also take the chair in Committee. When a member of the Working Committee is temporarily absent, his place may be taken by another Elected Member of the Delegation of the same party group as the absent member. A quorum exists for the Working Committee when at least three members are present. The vote of the Chairman shall decide equal divisions.
> The Working Committee is to take care of the Delegation's running affairs, and to treat with those matters which are referred to the Working Committee by the Delegation.

The Norwegian delegation limits the size of its working committee to three persons. At any given time, two parties have gone unrepresented. A similar policy has been followed in Iceland since 1958, and one party has been unrepresented. Denmark, Finland, and Sweden, on the other hand, include all Nordic Council parties in the working committees. Consequently, the Finnish working committee has had six or seven members; the chairman and vice-chairman act as a working subcommittee. On all the working committees, the parties represented have a single seat, except that the Social Democrats have two places on the Swedish committee, and the Speaker of the Danish Parliament, also a Social Democrat, serves as an additional member of the Danish committee.

By Statute in Sweden, by implication from the Statute in Finland, and by custom in the other three countries, the chairman of

[6] Law No. 170 of April 1, 1960, paragraphs 3 and 4.

the national delegation is also chairman of the working committee. Vice-chairmanships are also duplicated.

Each party selects its own working committee delegate. Once appointed, a member usually has tenure as long as his party retains its representation on the working committee and as long as the representative continues to be an elected member of the Nordic Council.

Not only is continuity high in the working committees, but its members are leaders in their home parliaments. Of the forty-six persons who served on Nordic Council delegation working committees during the seven years from 1953 to 1959, thirty-six were party chairmen or floor leaders, presiding officers of Parliament, or former cabinet members.

While Section 25 of the Rules of Procedure of the Nordic Council directs the working committees to concern themselves with "the organization of the Council's activities," it authorizes them only "to *consult* with the Presidium and with [each] other" in such matters (emphasis added). Section 22 of the Rules is much more direct and forceful in telling the Presidium that it "shall be responsible for the conduct of the Council's current activities" and "shall provide for the management of the . . . secretariats. . . ." This latter duty is also given the Presidium by the higher mandate of Article VIII of the Statute of the Nordic Council.

This statutory balance of power is somewhat altered in Finland and Sweden by the provisions there for the working committees to supervise the day-to-day work of the delegations and by the further authorization to the Finnish working committee to engage personnel other than the Secretary-General. Still, none of the national working committees has actually supervised the activities of the delegations on a daily basis.

The duty of each working committee to consult with the Presidium can ordinarily only be carried out by consulting with the national member of the Presidium. Usually this member can merely report to the working committee the decision which the Presidium has already reached—for example, as to the classification of expenses as joint or several, or as to the party complexion required of new members of Nordic Council committees. As to these latter, given the further application of rules of seniority or, in the case of Finland and Iceland, the possible existence of language disqualifications, there may be only one person left for the working committee to recommend to the delegation to fill the particular opening. By mutual tacit consent, the right to be consulted becomes the right to be kept informed.

The upshot is that routine decisions as to expenses, staff, and committee assignments are made by the national member of the Presidium on the advice of the Presidium and the Secretaries-General, and the latter conduct the running affairs of the delegations.

THE JOINT WORKING COMMITTEE

The Joint Working Committee is a separate organ of the Nordic Council, with powers in addition to those of the individual working committees. This singular constitutional status stems from custom, is enhanced by the fact that the Joint Committee automatically includes the members of the Presidium, and is consistent with the injunction of Section 25 of the Council's Rules of Procedure, that each working committee shall "consult with the Presidium and with the other working committees on questions concerning the organization of the Council's activities."

The Joint Working Committee has acted as the voice of the entire Council in some organizational matters. It met on November 2–3, 1952, to plan the first annual session. Since the 1954 session, the Joint Working Committee has assumed the task of drafting, promulgating, and amending the Directions for Committee Work. The standing committees have acquiesced in these Directions, and they have a validity comparable to that of the Rules of Procedure. Of course, the Council could revise or revoke the Directions.

Its failure to do so is an example of a tacit delegation of authority to the Joint Working Committee which is by now a venerable custom. The result is an increase in the power of the Presidium, acting through the Joint Working Committee, and a decrease in standing committee autonomy in matters of procedure.

Another function of the Joint Working Committee flows more from the accident of physical propinquity than from any juristic quality of jointness. It has been noted that the working committees are circumscribed in their discretion in making interim appointments to Nordic Council committees by the fact that such appointments are dependent on the simultaneous decisions of the other delegations. Section 25 of the Rules of Procedure directs the working committees to consult with one another; however, during the interim, such consultation is carried out by the Presidium or the Secretaries-General. Conceivably, the Joint Working Committee could convene during the interim to help the separate working committees better to perform their functions. It has not done so.

A different situation presents itself with those appointments to committees which are made at the annual sessions. Here the national delegations are all gathered at the same time and place, and, consequently, so are the five working committees. Thus, the spatial obstacle to joint consultation with which they are faced between sessions is removed.

The most important meeting of the Joint Working Committee takes place on the day before or the first day of each annual session. At this meeting, the Directions for Committee Work are adopted, and a package roster of proposed committee assignments is accepted. Without exception, the nominees have been elected unanimously and without debate at the first plenary meeting of an annual session.

The functions of the Joint Working Committee, then, are sessional and organizational: it formulates rules for the guidance of the standing committees, and assists the Council in allocating committee assignments. In each case, much groundwork has been laid by the national secretariats, in consultation with the Presidium and in consultation with the separate working committees and national delegations, particularly as to committee assignments. The process is a fluid one, but again the advantage lies with the smaller and better-informed organs, the Presidium and the Secretaries-General.

THE PRESIDIUM

Article V of the Statute of the Nordic Council directs the Council to choose a Presidium from among the elected members at each annual session, to consist of a President and four Vice-Presidents who are to serve until the next annual session. Section 7 of the Rules of Procedure of the Council adds the requirement that each country must be represented on the Presidium, as must "different political opinions."

The chairmen of the national delegations are automatically elected to the Presidium. This custom takes precedence over the written regulations. Thus, when the Icelandic delegation changed chairmen in 1957, and when the Danish delegation did the same in January, 1964, the old chairman stepped down from the Presidium—even though his statutory term had not expired and he was still an elected member of the Council—and was replaced by the new chairman.

Article VIII of the Statute empowers the Presidium to supervise the activities of the national secretariats. Section 22 of the Rules reiterates this mandate, and further makes the Presidium "responsible for the conduct of the Council's current activities" during the interim period. This section goes on to specify that each member of the Presidium is to undertake the "direct management" of his own national secretariat.

Article IX of the Statute authorizes the Presidium to "cause such studies to be made as it may deem necessary" with regard to matters formally submitted to the Council. In the original draft of this article, the national secretariats were to undertake studies and to determine the need for studies. At the request of the Norwegian government, this authority was transferred to the Presidium, in order to prevent the growth of a Nordic bureaucracy. The passive voice used in Article IX encompasses both Presidium stimulation of governmental research and Presidium-directed study by the secretariats, by Nordic Council committees, or by civil servants hired for special projects.

For a decade the Presidium was characterized by stability and by the political prominence of its members. Denmark, Norway, and Sweden had only two Presidium members from the time the Council was founded until 1964. Since 1964, the Presidium has experienced a complete turnover of membership, including two changes each for Denmark, Finland, and Norway.

In Sweden, the original member of the Presidium, Nils Herlitz, left the Nordic Council when he retired from the Swedish Parliament at the end of 1955. He was succeeded in January, 1956, by the leader of the Liberal party, Bertil Ohlin. Ohlin served for ten years before being replaced in 1966 by the Conservative Leif Cassel.

In Denmark (1953) and in Norway (1955), the original Presidium member left that post to become Prime Minister. The former, Hans Hedtoft, was replaced on the Presidium by the outgoing Prime Minister, the Moderate Liberal Erik Eriksen. Eriksen stepped down in 1964 so that he could devote more time to the upcoming parliamentary elections, as party leader. He was replaced by Harald Nielsen, also a member of the Moderate Liberal party, and charter elected member to the Nordic Council. Nielsen did not seek to retain his seat in the November, 1966, elections to the Danish Parliament.

As successor to Einar Gerhardsen, Nils Hønsvald served for eight years as the Norwegian member of the Presidium. Hønsvald had been a cabinet member, Vice-Speaker of the Norwegian Parliament, and chairman of the Labor party's group in Parliament. In 1964, his place was taken by John Lyng, then Conservative group leader in Parliament, and formerly Prime Minister for three weeks during the summer of 1963. Lyng became Foreign Minister in 1965, and was replaced on the Presidium by a leading Laborite, Trygve Bratteli.

Not only did the Danish and Norwegian members change in 1964, but the Icelandic Vice-President was also replaced. The present member of the Presidium from Iceland has held that office on previous occasions. He is Sigurdur Bjarnason, editor of *Morgunbladid,* the Conservative party's daily newspaper, and Speaker of the Lower Division of the Icelandic Parliament.

Finnish Presidium membership was unstable until 1960. Two of the three men who served alternated at home as Prime Minister. (One of the Icelandic Presidium members also stepped down from that post to become Prime Minister.) From 1960 to 1966, the Finnish member of the Presidium was the Social Democrat Karl-August Fagerholm, former Prime Minister and long-time Speaker of the Finnish Parliament. Fagerholm retired and was succeeded briefly by Kaarlo Pitsinki, chairman of the Social Democratic party. Pitsinki left Parliament to become a provincial governor and was replaced on the Presidium by another Social Democrat, Eino Sirén.

Without exception, the Council-in-session has elected the chairman of the host delegation as President of the Nordic Council. The sessions are held in rotation in the capitals, and the presidency has thus been successively Danish, Finnish, Norwegian, Swedish, and Icelandic. The President of the Nordic Council is *primus inter pares.* Each annual session is opened by the outgoing President and closed by the incoming President. Otherwise, the speakership is rotated among the President and Vice-Presidents during a session. The President takes the chair at meetings of the Presidium. These meetings are informal, however, and the chairman does not dominate them.

Section 22 of the Rules of Procedure permits the Presidium to reach unanimous decisions without actually meeting. In more routine activities, particularly those regarding their own national secretariats, the members of the Presidium act individually, without mutual consultation. Apart from the annual sessions, the Presidium meets three or four times a year. Between meetings, liaison is maintained by the Secretaries-General.

The functions of the Presidium are numerous and impressive. They include the following:

1. To allocate Nordic Council expenses to the member delegations, within the limits set by the Statute and Rules of Procedure of the Council.

2. To supervise the national secretariats, jointly and severally.

3. To receive communications from pressure groups.

4. To request that studies of particular matters be made by the governments, by the secretariats, or by Nordic Council committees.

5. To establish and call meetings of committees during the interim.

6. To allocate vacant seats on Nordic Council committees, in consultation with the national delegations and with the working committees.

7. To receive reports from the governments on the steps being taken to implement Nordic Council recommendations, and to stimulate greater efforts when these seem called for.

8. To supervise the public relations activities of the Nordic Council.

9. To act as the procedural traffic policeman of the Nordic Council, as to matters introduced and reports submitted for Council consideration.

THE NATIONAL SECRETARIATS

There is no central Nordic Council headquarters. Article VIII of the Statute of the Nordic Council directs each national delegation to "appoint a Secretary-General and other staff members," and implies that the Secretaries will collaborate with each other.

Section 8 of the Rules of Procedure provides that "the Secretary of a session [Chief Clerk] shall be the Secretary-General of the delegation in whose country the session is held." Originally, it was thought that the last Secretary of a session would continue as chief Secretary-General until the next session, as had been the case with the Nordic Inter-Parliamentary Union. Such a provision was deleted from the Statute as proposed in 1952. Thus, there are five juridically equal secretariats, each established by its parent national delegation.

Hans Hedtoft wanted a strong Nordic Council and a prominent Danish Secretary-General. He chose the executive director of the Danish Norden Society, Frantz Wendt, formerly lecturer in history at the University of Copenhagen. Wendt was the only full-time Secretary-General during the first few formative years of the Council.

The first Secretary-General of the Finnish Nordic Council delegation was Ragnar Meinander, a civil servant in the Ministry of Education, who served from January 1, 1956, to May 30, 1957. Meinander had been secretary to the Nordic Cultural Commission. A Swede-Finn, he was active in the Swedish People's party—the only Nordic Council Secretary-General with such open political affiliation. It is part of the Swedish People's party's program to foster the closest possible contact with Sweden and the rest of Scandinavia.

Meinander's appointment was considered by some of the Finnish Nordic Council delegation members to be political, and the position of Secretary-General was declared open. Fifteen applicants presented themselves. After numerous postponements, a new Secretary-General was elected on May 16, 1957. The vote in the national delegation was divided six to six, and the new Secretary-General was chosen over the old by lot. He is Eiler Hultin, a jurist whose native tongue is Finnish. Hultin had no prior connection with Nordic cooperation.

The Chief Clerk of the Icelandic Parliament serves as Secretary-General to the Icelandic delegation to the Nordic Council. The first Icelandic Secretary-General, Jón Sigurdsson, retired as Chief Clerk on July 1, 1956, but retained his Nordic Council position until he died on October 31, 1957. The present Secretary-General is Fridjón Sigurdsson.

Icelandic communications with the other national secretariats have not been extensive. Nordic matters take little of the Chief Clerk's time, apart from the annual sessions themselves and the immediate preparations for them.

There is some ambiguity as to who served as Secretary-General to the Norwegian Nordic Council delegation before and during the first session of the Council in February, 1953. The official record of the first session lists Bjarne Solheim as the delegation secretary—and it was Solheim who worked with the other Secretaries-General in preparing for the session. On the other hand, the report on the first session submitted by the Norwegian delegation to its parent body, the Norwegian Parliament, gives Erik Nord as First Secretary, and Bjarne Solheim as one of three others who also served the delegation at the session. What is clear is that all of the delegation Secretaries were supplied from the staff of the Foreign Ministry. In any event, Erik Nord served as Secretary-General to the Norwegian delegation from 1954 to 1957, inclusive.

In April, 1958, the present Secretary-General, Einar Løchen, was appointed. Løchen, a former Fellow of the Christian Michelsen Institute (Bergen), follows scholarly pursuits in the field of international organization, but was not active in applied Nordic cooperation prior to his 1958 appointment. He retained active contact with the Foreign Ministry, serving until 1962 as the Foreign Minister's permanent representative to the Committee of Ministers of the Council of Europe. Løchen holds his Nordic Council position on a full-time basis—which was not the case with his predecessors, who also served the parliamentary Committee on Foreign Affairs, the Norwegian delegation to the Council of Europe, and the Norwegian NATO parliamentarians.

The Secretary-General of the Swedish delegation to the Nordic Council is Gustaf Petrén, Doctor of Jurisprudence and Docent in the University of Stockholm. Petrén holds the permanent rank of judge in the Swedish civil service system and is a member of the International Commission of Jurists. He was not active in Nordic cooperation prior to becoming Secretary-General.

The Swedish Secretary-General is responsible both to the Swedish Nordic Council delegation as Secretary-General, and to the Parliament as a whole, as head of the Nordic Council chancellery. Conversely, he has an area of independence from either. He could not be discharged, for example, by the delegation acting unilaterally —as the first Finnish Secretary-General was replaced in 1957. A complaint against him would have to be considered by the parliamentary Committee on Banking, following established procedures. No other Nordic Council Secretary-General is so secure in his position, whether as regards the government, the Parliament, or the Nordic Council national delegation.

Since December, 1956, the Swedish delegation has had the services of a half-time administrative assistant, recruited from the Nordic affairs desk of the Foreign Ministry. The dual role provides a convenient liaison between the chancellery of the Nordic Council and the Ministry.

Each national secretariat has its own housekeeping chores, which include bookkeeping, archival work, staff supervision, and arrangements for meetings of the national delegation and working committee, and of the Presidium, Nordic Council committees, and annual sessions when they take place in the given capital. Permanent committee secretaries and civil servants who have been retained on an *ad hoc* basis to prepare reports on matters on the agenda of a pending session are attached administratively to the Nordic Council secretariat of their own nationality.[7]

The Secretaries-General distribute pamphlets and press releases, give speeches, work with educators, and orient members of Parliament. Finally, they follow the implementation of Nordic Council recommendations by the governments at all levels of the administrative structure.

On the basis of an informal division of labor, the Danish Secretary-General takes considerable responsibility for Nordic Council public relations. Frantz Wendt is the only current Secretary-General with extensive pre-Council experience in the field of Scandinavian cooperation. He tends to look beyond the Nordic Council to new forms of Nordic integration, and is thus concerned with molding the Nordic image. Wendt has written a book on the Council and numerous articles of a historical and descriptive nature.

Much of the work of the Finnish secretariat is devoted to bridging the language barrier. The majority of Finnish members of Parliament do not understand Swedish, much less Danish or Norwegian. (A shortened Finnish version of the record of each Nordic Council annual session is prepared for the Finnish-speaking members of Parliament.) Or, if they read Swedish, they may not speak it comfortably.

[7] See the Instructions for Joint Civil Servants promulgated by the Presidium on June 14, 1963, and reproduced in Olof Wallmén, *Nordiska rådet och nordiskt samarbete* (Stockholm: Norstedt, 1966), pp. 130–31.

As a result of recent impulses from the Finnish government, the climate surrounding the Finnish delegation and secretariat has undergone a change. Increased and more meaningful Scandinavian cooperation is now a part of the official program of the Finnish government. New techniques of implementing cooperation are being developed. The Finnish Nordic Council secretariat is in a key position to coordinate these efforts. On September 30, 1960, the then Finnish Prime Minister, V. J. Sukselainen, formerly Nordic Council President, issued a directive which named the Nordic Council Secretary-General as a member of a new coordinating committee for Nordic Council matters (described in Chapter 5), composed otherwise of senior administrative officials. In May, 1963, the secretariat was made a chancellery of Parliament.

The Secretary-General of the Norwegian delegation to the Nordic Council does not have the independence from the government that the other four Secretaries enjoy. The others are responsible solely to their respective parliaments; the Norwegian Secretaries-General have always come from and retained contact with the Norwegian Foreign Ministry; those who have left the Nordic Council secretariat have returned to the Foreign Office. Some of the secretarial tasks have in fact been carried out by the office of the Prime Minister. Moreover, the political climate in Norway, whether ministerial or parliamentary, is not conducive to Nordic activism. Thus, propagandistic efforts, such as those of the Danish secretariat, would be out of place and would probably backfire.

Furthermore, the Norwegian Parliament is more accustomed to clerical than professional assistance in its committee work, and this attitude carried over to the Nordic Council secretariat. In recommending adherence to the Nordic Council Statute in 1952, the Foreign Ministry of Norway told the Parliament that "the Secretaries should for the most part have functions corresponding to those of parliamentary officials in the participating countries." [8] Thus, extensive investigations, such as those carried out or supervised by the Swedish secretariat, are not expected of the Norwegian Secretary-General. Nor would the small size of the staff permit a great deal of research.

In 1965, the Norwegian secretariat became secretary to the

[8] *St. prp.* (Stortingsproposisjon), 118/1952, p. 2. This was the government bill which introduced the Nordic Council Statute for consideration by the Norwegian Parliament.

Judging Committee for the Nordic Council Prize in Music, in an attempt to distribute the secretarial work of the Council more widely. The prize is awarded every third year.

The Swedish secretariat has primary responsibility for legal questions in the Nordic Council. The Swedish Secretary-General has published several articles in professional journals describing the structure and operation of the Council, and he represented the Nordic Council in Rome at the 1959 meeting of the Institut international pour l'unification du droit privé. Dr. Petrén also takes care of the more technical aspects of the preparatory work for Presidium, committee, and sessional meetings. In collaboration with the other national secretariats, the Swedish office acts as secretary to the Judging Committee for the Nordic Council Literary Prize, which is bestowed at each annual session.

At first, each national secretariat was responsible for editing the record which emerged from a session in its own capital. It was found to be inefficient to have the reports prepared by a different person and printed in a different place each year; and this was a severe seasonal burden to place on the most recent host Secretary-General. In 1957, a permanent editor was appointed—Tryggve Byström, of Stockholm. Byström had previously edited the record of the third annual session (Stockholm, 1955). In 1962, he was replaced by another Stockholmer, Olof Wallmén. Wallmén is not formally attached to the Swedish secretariat, but his administrative connection with the Council is through that office.

In addition to the annual record, the Nordic Council's permanent editor is responsible for *Nytt från Nordiska rådet* (initially, in 1955 and 1956, called *Meddelande från Nordiska rådet*), a comprehensive mimeographed collection of articles and editorials taken mostly from Scandinavian newspapers. The clippings concern Nordic cooperation. They are gathered—and, in the case of Finnish and Icelandic sources, translated—by the Swedish diplomatic corps in the several capitals. *Nytt från Nordiska rådet* comes out about twelve times a year. The editor also supervises the preparation of *Nordisk Udredningsserie,* a series of reports on particular topics of Scandinavian cooperation which the Nordic Council has been publishing since 1960. Finally, he edits a periodic calendar of Nordic Council events.

By its own decision, the board of editors of *Nordisk Kontakt*—a journal of Scandinavian parliamentary affiairs sponsored by the

Nordic Council—has gradually shifted its work to the Swedish members. The board is elected by the Council, mostly from among the elected members. The chief editor is also in Stockholm, and the auditors are two Swedish elected members of the Nordic Council. Since 1960, the secretarial work of the journal has been taken care of by the Swedish Nordic Council secretariat.

The Secretaries-General of the Danish, Finnish, Norwegian, and Swedish national delegations are in almost constant contact with one another, by mail, telephone, and in person. As earlier stated, each secretariat serves its own national delegation. The all-Nordic tasks—those which would have been delegated to a central secretariat if one had been established—are divided as indicated between the Danish and Swedish secretariats, but with the latter gradually assuming an ever greater share of the growing work of the Council. The Swedish secretariat now has eight full-time employees, twice as many as either the Danish or Finnish offices, which are in turn larger than the Norwegian.

Fear of the possible creation of a Nordic bureaucracy led to the rejection of the idea of an all-Nordic Council secretariat. The practical result has been to create a larger and far stronger Nordic civil service than probably would have been the case if there had been a single, central organ. An all-Scandinavian Nordic Council Secretary-General in the Danish pattern would have been resented in Norway. An all-Scandinavian secretariat on the Norwegian model would have been much less active than the *de facto* Dano-Swedish common secretariat. Even an all-Scandinavian secretariat like the Swedish secretariat would not have had that advantage which derives from having an on-the-spot contact man of the same nationality as the Parliament and government with which he must deal.

COMMITTEES

Standing committees are the workhorses of the Council. All proposals are referred to them, and final consideration is always based upon a committee report.

The time available during session is inadequate for deliberation in keeping with the high standards of preparation prevalent in Scandinavia. This pressure fosters excessive reliance on staff and experts and gives rise to the need for interim deliberations.

The Council set up interim committees of limited scope in 1953,

1956, and 1957. Since 1954, the Council has regularly authorized the Presidium to do the same during the interim—an authorization which the Presidium used in 1955, 1956, 1957, and 1962. Permanent interim committees of general competence were established by the Council in 1955 (Judiciary), 1958 (Social Policy), 1959 (Economic Matters), and 1963 (Cultural Affairs). At the 1964 session, the nine-man interim committees were superseded by the full standing committees.

Standing Committees

Until 1964, the standing committees met only during annual session, with rare exception. At the first three annual sessions, the Council established four standing committees: the Cultural Affairs Committee, the Committee on Judiciary, the Committee on Social Policy, and the Committee on Economic Matters and Communications. Since the fourth session, when Finland first participated, there have been five standing committees, including separate Committees on Economic Matters and Communications. Each elected member serves on one standing committee and only one.

Section 10 of the Rules of Procedure specifies that elections to standing committees shall aim at "diversified representation." This has been construed to encompass both national and party diversity.

Iceland has one member of each standing committee. The other four countries are equally represented, with three members on the Committees on Judiciary, Social Policy, Cultural Affairs, and Communications, and four members on the Committee on Economic Matters. The Economic Matters Committee has seventeen members, while the others each have thirteen. (Following similar principles prior to 1956, there were three thirteen-member standing committees and one fourteen-member standing committee, the last with two Icelandic members.)

National equality in standing committee offices is complete, even including Icelandic parity. Each standing committee is chaired by an elected member from a different country, and each country has one vice-chairmanship. The chairman and vice-chairman of a given standing committee are always from different countries. It was to provide an additional chairmanship that the number of committees was increased to five when Finland joined the Council.

Party diversification has also been attained. Of all the thirteen- and fourteen-member committees, there is only one case between 1953 and 1960 where there were fewer than five or more than eight members on a given standing committee from either the Socialist parties as a whole or from the bourgeois parties as a whole.

In the allocation of standing committee offices, party diversification has varied. Until 1955, the chairmanships were divided evenly between Socialist and non-Socialist parties. From 1956 to 1961, the bourgeois parties had four of the five chairmanships, except for 1959, when they had all five, of whom four were Conservatives. In 1962, the balance was again restored, with two Social Democrats, one Liberal, one Agrarian, and one Conservative serving as standing committee chairmen. The two-to-three ratio of Socialists and non-Socialists has since been retained.

Seventeen different persons filled the five standing committee chairmanships during the first eight sessions—two Danes, three Swedes, three Finns, four Norwegians, and five Icelanders. Continuity is in inverse proportion to the number who have served. Eleven of these seventeen were members of national working committes. On nine occasions when a person stepped down from a standing committee chairmanship, it was because he had left the Council. Two of the three chairmen who vacated their positions while continuing as elected members did so because they were chosen to serve on the Council Presidium.

Continuity in standing committee membership is mixed (see chart 5). In 1959, for example, each standing committee had three

CHART 5.

NUMBER OF TERMS ON SAME STANDING COMMITTEE PREVIOUSLY
SERVED BY STANDING COMMITTEE MEMBERS AT THE SEVENTH ANNUAL
SESSION OF THE NORDIC COUNCIL, 1959

| | Number of terms previously served: | | | | | | | |
	0	1	2	3	4	5	6	*Total*
Judiciary	4	1	2	1	0	2	3	13
Cultural Affairs	3	5	2	1	0	0	2	13
Social Policy	4	3	0	1	1	2	2	13
Communications	5	1	4	3	x	x	x	13
Economic Matters	4	4	4	0	1	2	2	17

x = The Standing Committee on Communications did not become a separate committee until the fourth annual session to five neophytes and two or three members who had served on the committee at all previous sessions.

Interim Committees

The evolution of interim committee activity is the most striking example of growth among the Council's organs, comparable only to that of the national secretariats. Originally, the Council relied on *ad hoc* interim committees, but gradually built up a set of regular interim committees of general competence. Until they were replaced by the standing committees in 1964, the interim committees came to perform more and more of the substantial work of the Council.

The 1953 Committee on Equal Protection of the Law for Nordic Citizens was a forerunner of the Interim Committee on Judiciary which was founded in 1955. The 1955 and 1956 Special Committee on Uniform Labor Laws and 1956 and 1957 Special Committee for a Common Medical Labor Market were precursors to the Interim Committee on Social Policy which was launched at the 1958 session. The Interim Committee on Economic Matters had no such predecessor, but was created in 1959 to compensate for the failure to form a common Nordic market.

The Nordic Cultural Commission, described in Chapter 5, did much of the work which otherwise might have been performed by a Nordic Council interim committee. The secretary to the Nordic Council Standing Committee on Cultural Affairs served on the staff of the commission, and about half of the ten legislative members of the commission attended the Nordic Council as elected members. This overlap of function and personnel explains why no interim committee was set up until 1963.

On July 2, 1962, the Presidium decided to establish an Interim Committee on Cultural Affairs. Each national delegation except the Icelandic appointed members to the committee, which met on January 17, 1963, to consider appropriate items on the agenda for the upcoming session.

A significant portion of the Norwegian delegation to the 1963 session in Oslo opposed the continuation of the nine-man Interim Committee on Cultural Affairs. Håkon Johnsen, Norwegian Laborite and charter elected member to the Council, moved that the creation of the interim committee be postponed one year. He argued as follows:

The question of a cultural nine-man committee has been raised in the Council's Cultural Affairs Committee for several Sessions. Its creation was posed time after time . . . , but each time the Cultural Affairs Committee said that [it] was not necessary, because one had the Nordic Cultural Commission, which was fully utilizable for work between Sessions. . . .

Now it is argued that a new situation has arisen out of the reorganization of the Nordic Cultural Commission, and when one did not get the Committee on Cultural Affairs to go in for a cultural nine-man committee, then one used the general authorization which the Presidium had, to set up a cultural nine-man committee, which has had one meeting, at which the Norwegian representatives said that they would take up the entire question when the Council met in Oslo.[9]

Johnsen was supported in debate by four of his countrymen. One of these was another Laborite, while the others were from the Agrarian, Conservative, and Christian People's parties. By voice vote, the Presidium's proposal for constituting the committee carried, defeating the dilatory motion, and the Interim Committee on Cultural Affairs was perpetuated.

As mentioned in Chapter 2, the governments set up a Nordic Traffic Committee in 1957, on the recommendation of the Nordic Council. It was composed of two members of Parliament from Denmark, Finland, Norway, and Sweden, and one from Iceland. The committee had a rotating chairmanship and met about three times a year. On January 1, 1965, the committee was radically reconstructed pursuant to Nordic Council Recommendation 30/1964. The committee secretaries became the members of the committee on that date, and parliamentary membership was abolished in the face of year-round operation by the Nordic Council Standing Committee on Communications. Prior to this transformation, four to six of the parliamentary members attended the annual sessions of the Nordic Council. Three members of the Nordic Traffic Committee were usually members of the Nordic Council Standing Committee on Communications. Even though the Nordic Traffic Committee was established by the governments, it functioned partly as an interim committee of the Nordic Council. This dual status was given explicit recognition by the governments and the Presidium in 1962.

[9] *1963 Record*, p. 222.

Each of the four regular Nordic Council interim committees had two representatives from the four larger countries, and one from Iceland. No one served on more than one of these nine-man committees at the same time. Party balance on the nine-man committees was comparable to that found on the standing committees: there was a rough equality in distribution of seats between the Socialist and bourgeois parties.

In contrast with the standing committees, continuity in membership on the nine-man committees was extremely high. This was accomplished by retaining members on the committee when they were absent from the session, or when they were no longer elected members of the Council but only alternate delegates. Nor were the interim committees strictly limited to their parent standing committee in finding members. Members leaving an interim committee usually retired from the Council at the same time.

Until 1963, the interim committees were autonomous in choosing their officers. The vice-chairman of an interim committee was always from a different country than the chairman, but the nine-man committees did not otherwise impose any restrictions on themselves as to nationality, party, or seniority. In recent years, the chairmen of the Interim Committees on Judiciary and on Social Policy were either Danes or Swedes. In fact, two of the three interim committee chairmen were usually Swedes.

There was little turnover in office. From 1953 to 1961, three Danes, three Norwegians, and two Swedes served as chairmen of Nordic Council interim committees of one kind or another.

With the creation of the fourth interim committee in 1963, it became possible to effect equal national distribution of chairmanships among the four larger nations. Two of the chairmen were Social Democrats, one was a Conservative, and one a member of the Swedish People's party of Finland.

Committee Staff

Nordic Council committee secretaries are civil servants from the administrative organs of the member countries. At the first five annual sessions, the secretaries changed from year to year, and did not reappear when the session returned to their own capital. In 1958, the turnover system was abandoned. Each standing committee now has a permanent part-time secretary, who serves on a year-round basis. Until 1964, the same person served both standing and interim committee, including the Nordic Traffic Committee when it functioned in that capacity.

The secretaries are paid on a part-time basis, except during the annual sessions. Apart from the sessions, the secretaries are expected to devote only a couple of days per month to committee work, other than the secretary to the Social Policy Committee, who is employed on a two-thirds time basis. The secretaries' work is concentrated at the times when the committees meet—normally for two days three or four times a year. The secretaries have only occasional contact with committee members except during formal meetings, but are in regular communication with the Secretaries-General, who set timetables and indicate appropriate topics for interim consideration. The secretaries prepare committee recommendations in consultation with the Secretaries-General.

In studying matters which are on the agenda of the Nordic Council, the committees do not normally carry out extensive independent investigation, but attempt rather to digest the findings of other investigatory bodies. Judge Knud Thestrup, Danish Conservative chairman of the nine-man Nordic Council Interim Committee on Judiciary, noted that:

> . . . technical questions are the chore of departments [and] scholars, and are completely outside the work which a nine-man committee, which meets very briefly and relatively infrequently, is in a position to direct itself to. . . . The work of the nine-man committees is to take initiative, to supervise the work carried out by the governments. . . .[10]

An exception to this rule has been the Committee on Social Policy. As secretary to the various social welfare interim committees from 1955 to 1961, Sven-Hugo Ryman was responsible for all of the Council's research on the common medical labor market.

The purpose of interim study was to make the standing committees more effective in considering the matters before them at the annual sessions. In this they have succeeded, within the bounds imposed by limitations of time and staff. The opportunity which the committees have to orient themselves during the interim reduces their dependence on committee staff and governmental experts. The growth of interim committee activity has increased the over-all effectiveness of the Nordic Council, but has not altered the

[10] *1961 Record,* pp. 177–78.

basic structure of the organization, nor of its relationship to the governments.

APPRAISAL

The recurrent characteristic of Nordic Council power distribution is centralization in the Presidium and delegation to the Secretaries-General. The members of the Presidium are the chairmen of their respective national delegations and working committees. Furthermore, they are key figures in their home parliaments. As a result of this symbiosis of power and prestige, it can be said that the Presidium *is* the Council. The reduction is particularly evident during interim periods. The Presidium influences the choice of its own replacements, selects the standing committee chairmen, and, to a lesser extent, appoints committee members. The Presidium can call interim meetings of committees and fix their agendas. The Presidium arranges upcoming sessions; the choice of problem areas for special Council emphasis at the annual sessions is made by the Presidium in consultation with the governments. At the first annual session (Copenhagen, 1953), the chairmen of the standing committees formulated their own Directions for Committee Work, in consultation with the Presidium. At the second session (Oslo, 1954), and ever since, the Presidium has used the Joint Working Committee as a medium for the promulgation of the Directions, which have grown ever more detailed. This is an instance of centralization of power. Finally, the Presidium is the sole official conduit to the outside world, and represents the entire Council in following the progress of the Council's recommendations in the administrative hoppers of the national governments.

Some dialogue, incapable of precise measurement, goes on between Presidium member and working committee, between Presidium member and national delegation. Parliamentary leaders in Scandinavia are adept at sounding opinion, and informal accommodation is generally typical of Scandinavian political life. Nevertheless, Presidium members speak more to advise than to inquire, ask more for information than opinion. For example, at the meeting of the Joint Working Committee on the day after the end of the first annual session of the Nordic Council, the members of the Presidium dominated the discussion—particularly those from Denmark, Norway, and Sweden (Finland not yet having joined the Council). The Secretaries-General were next in extent of participation, the ordinary working committee members last. It was at this meeting that the procedural experience of the first session was digested.

Neither the governments nor the parliaments need acquiesce in presidential hegemony any longer than they wish. The fact is that the tasks so far assumed by the Nordic Council have been more appropriate for disposition by civil servants than by politicians. If the Nordic Council should ever be given supranational powers, there is no reason why it could not come to function more like the national parliaments.

While the Presidium has gathered the reins of Nordic Council power, it has put them in the hands of the Secretaries-General. The Swedish Secretary-General has distinguished between those duties relating to the national delegations and those relating to the Council as a whole:

> The most import[ant] tasks of the national secretariats are not however confined to—or even primarily connected with—the activities of the national delegations. Probably the most responsible task of the secretariats is that of carrying out their joint responsibilities within the Council.[11]

It is these joint duties which are not equally divided among the secretariats. ". . . [T]he shared labor must for the most part be placed on the Danish and Swedish Secretariats as well as, in some degree, on the Finnish Secretariat." [12] These duties consist of advising the Presidium in the selection of members to fill Council posts, supervising the interim activities of the committees, coordinating the work of governmental agencies working with Nordic Council recommendations, and planning and arranging for the meetings of the Presidium and for the annual sessions. It is clear that these duties parallel those of the Presidium.

The routine preparations for a session fall upon the host secretariat. Subject matter preparation is placed primarily on the Swedish secretariat. Until 1962, the supervision of staff personnel for Nordic Council interim committees fell solely upon the Danish and Swedish secretariats, inasmuch as permanent Secretaries were found only in Copenhagen and Stockholm. During the interim, committees are more an adjunct to the secretariats than a competi-

[11] Gustaf Petrén, "The Nordic Council: A Unique Factor in International Law," *Nordisk Tidsskrift for International Ret,* XXIX, No. 4 (1959), 355.

[12] *Bankoutskottets utlåtande* 15/1957, p. 9.

tor. The Secretaries-General set the agendas and in some cases even write the committee reports. They are also instrumental in finding suitable new topics for Council consideration.

The most delicate and important task performed by the Secretaries-General is to follow the actions of the governmental agencies in Nordic Council matters, and to stimulate them when necessary. The Presidium has urged that additional staff be provided so that this work can be done more effectively.

The Secretaries-General are the only decision makers who are concerned with Nordic matters on a full-time, permanent basis. Collectively, they have a monopoly on the knowledge which the politicians need in order to operate. This expertise often carries with it the power to decide which issues shall be brought to the forefront for consideration. Thus, with regard to the domestic application of studies emerging from Council investigations, Petrén notes that "often the real initiative in such cases is taken by the secretariat of the Council." [13]

Still, the Secretaries-General are in frequent contact with the members of the Presidium and, less often, with the working committee and other members of the national delegation. Residual power rests successively with the Presidium, the working committees, the national delegations, the parliaments—and, ultimately, with the peoples. It is a reflection of the weakness of the Council that its power is exercised by civil servants.

By tempering enthusiasm with tact, the secretariats have kept the confidence which their many masters have placed in them. Yet, one goal of the Nordic Council Secretaries-General is self-immolating: to convince the governments that Nordic Council affairs are important enough to be run by politicians. This is Frantz Wendt's goal, and was that of Hans Hedtoft. The need for increased governmental participation in the work of the Council has been one of the recurrent themes of Nordic Council self-evaluation. Meanwhile, Petrén's method, taken from Nils Herlitz, will continue to function: it consists of the steady accretion of concrete advances in specific matters of cooperation. (The two emphases are by no means mutually exclusive.) Politicians are used to break occasional log jams, but for the most part the civil servants can carry on independently—and they do.

[13] Gustaf Petrén, "Sweden," in Kenneth Lindsay (ed.), *European Assemblies* (London: Stevens, 1960), p. 203.

Chapter Four

FROM PROPOSAL TO

RECOMMENDATION—PROCEDURE

IN THE NORDIC COUNCIL

Elected members to the Council may offer proposals for consideration by the Council at the annual sessions, as may the governments.
The latter also submit memoranda on action taken on recommendations which the Council has made at earlier sessions, and transmit reports on Scandinavian cooperation. These matters are referred to the standing committees. Committee proposals provide
the only basis for debate and decision on second reading. Positive
decisions take the form of recommendations to the governments
(see chart 6).

SUMMONING A SESSION

Annual (Ordinary) Sessions

Article IV of the Statute of the Nordic Council states that the
"Council shall meet once a year on such date as it may decide
(ordinary session)." As required by this mandate, the Council has
met each year since 1953.

Six days, commencing on a week end, is the normal duration of
an annual session. Each session consists of one or two days of
general debate, one day of committee hearings, and three or
three-and-a-half days of debate on second reading. Prior to 1965,
the standard length of a session was seven days, including a second
day of committee hearings. Indeed, the initial sessions were some-

CHART 6.

How a Proposal Becomes a Recommendation

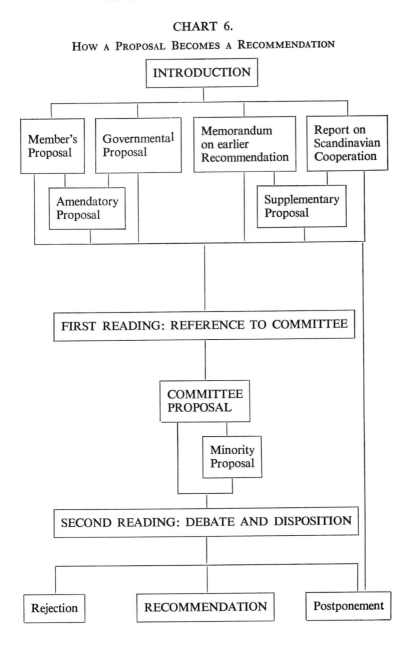

what longer, lasting from eight to ten days. Despite the increased work load, the six-day period now seems to be adequate, partly because of the rationalization of Council procedures and partly because of the increased use of interim committees.

Article IV of the Statute further requires that "ordinary sessions shall be held in one of the capitals of the countries, as decided by the Council." The sessions have been held successively in Copenhagen, Helsinki (starting in 1957), Oslo, Stockholm, and Reykjavik (starting in 1960).

Section 1(1) of the Rules of Procedure of the Council provides that the "Council may . . . leave it to the Presidium to fix the time for the opening of a session." In practice, the Council sets an approximate time for the next session, and then authorizes the Presidium to fix the exact date. Except for 1954 and 1958 through 1960, the sessions have been held during the winter, most frequently in February. The 1967 session is scheduled for the first week in April.

Section 1(1) of the Rules also provides that "In special circumstances, the Presidium may, with the consent of all the delegations, fix a time and a place for the session which is different from that which the Council has fixed." In an effort to coordinate Council deliberations with European free trade area negotiations, the 1958 session was postponed from January 27 to October 26, and then delayed a second time until November 9. (November was also used for the 1959 session. To make the return to winter sessions less precipitous, the 1960 session—abbreviated to four days—was held in July.) In 1962, the session in Helsinki originally scheduled for February was postponed until March because of unanticipated elections in Finland.

Section 1(3) of the Rules of Procedure instructs the Presidium to advise "the governments and elected members and their deputies . . . of the time and place for a session three months before it begins." The Presidium has met this deadline each year, except when last-minute postponements have made it impossible.

Article IX of the Statute of the Nordic Council directs the Presidium to "send the pertinent documents to the governments and members well before the session." Section 3(1) of the Rules of Procedure specifies that "governmental proposals and member's proposals, together with such studies as the Presidium may have found necessary, as well as memoranda and reports, shall be forwarded to the governments, members and deputy delegates as soon as possible and not later than three weeks before the session begins."

The secretariats are hampered in meeting the three-week deadline because some of the incoming documents—particularly memoranda—are tardy. In practice, the documents are sent out in batches progressively less than twenty-one days before the start of a session.

Extraordinary Sessions

Article IV of the Statute of the Nordic Council provides that "additional sessions shall be held when the Council so decides, or when requested by at least two governments or at least twenty-five elected members (extraordinary session)." Section 1(2) of the Rules of Procedure specifies that

> . . . If at least two governments or at least twenty-five elected members desire an extraordinary session to be convened, they shall submit a written request to that effect to the Presidium. Unless the Council has decided otherwise, the extraordinary session shall be held in such place and begin at such time as the Presidium may fix, if possible in consultation with the delegations.

No extraordinary sessions have been called, although the Presidium was authorized to call one before the 1959 session, if it should appear necessary in order to consider the possible formation of a common Nordic market as a regional unit in a new European free trade area.

Extraordinary sessions need not be held in one of the capitals of the member nations. It was felt that the circumstances giving rise to the need for an extraordinary session might at the same time preclude holding it in Scandinavia.

Section 3(3) of the Rules states that "extraordinary sessions . . . shall deal only with such matters as the Council has been convened to consider. All documents shall be circulated as soon as possible." However, Section 3(4) goes on to provide that "Regardless of the provisions of this section, the Council may decide, by a majority of two-thirds, to admit a matter for consideration."

INTRODUCTION OF MATTERS FOR COUNCIL CONSIDERATION

Governmental Proposals and Member's Proposals [1]

Article IX of the Statute of the Nordic Council authorizes "Each government and every member . . . to submit a matter to the Council by written application to the Presidium." Section 2(3) of the Rules of Procedure requires that a "member's proposal or a governmental proposal shall contain a proposal for a Council decision, except that a governmental proposal may merely contain a request for a statement of views."

Pursuant to Section 3(1) of the Rules, member's proposals and governmental proposals "must be submitted to a secretariat not later than two months before an ordinary session begins in order to be eligible for consideration by that session." Proposals have been submitted as early as the preceding session.

Section 3(1) further provides that the Presidium may reduce the two-month period to one month, "provided that this does not materially impair a necessary study." At first, the period of grace was granted automatically and was evidenced solely by the inclusion of the penumbral matter in the agenda. There were twelve such instances in 1955 and ten in 1956. In 1957, a new phrase was added to Section 3(1), limiting the Presidium's dispensation to "special cases." Since then, fewer proposals have been introduced in the period from one to two months before each session.

Section 3(4) of the Rules empowers the Council to waive all time requirements by a two-thirds vote. However, except for one governmental proposal, Item 7/1953, introduced just prior to the first annual session—before the Rules of Procedure were in effect—no matters have been introduced less than one month before the opening of an annual session. Some question arises from the fact that no dates were included on several proposals at the first and second sessions. Moreover, even when a date is given, it often indicates only the month, and in any event refers only to the time of signature by the author, which is not necessarily the same as the date of introduction through submission to a national secretariat. This lack of clarity effectively extends the discretionary authority

[1] The data upon which the observations in this section are based are tabulated in the author's unpublished doctoral dissertation, "The Nordic Council: An Institutional Analysis" (University of California [Berkeley], 1961), pp. 182–201.

of the Presidium and secretariats, as it prevents the Council from exercising control over dates of introduction.

Out of 215 proposals introduced during the first ten years of the Council, the governments were responsible for 21, or about 10 per cent (see chart 7). Seventeen of these—including all prior to 1959—used the permissive language of Section 2(3) of the Rules, quoted above, to ask the Council merely for a statement of views.

CHART 7.

NUMBER OF ITEMS OFFERED FOR CONSIDERATION AT EACH ANNUAL SESSION, 1953-62

| | Annual session in: | | | | | | | | | | |
	1953	1954	1955	1956	1957	1958	1959	1960	1961	1962	*Total*
Member's Proposals	6	15	22	19	25	28	19	17	17	26	194
Governmental Proposals	1	2	1	2	3	5	1	0	2	4	21
Amendatory Proposals	1	0	1	2	2	1	2	0	3	3	15
Supplementary Proposals	0	2	3	3	8	8	8	1	7	20	60
Subtotal	8	19	27	26	38	42	30	18	29	53	290
Memoranda	—	11	36	48	60	70	70	9	90	86	480
Reports	12	6	5	10	9	8	11	2	9	9	81
Postponed Items	—	0	11	8	5	3	8	8	12	13	68
Reports from Council Organs	—	2	1	3	3	5	4	5	5	5	33
Total	20	38	80	95	115	128	123	42	145	166	952

Four governmental proposals (Items B 3/1959, B 1/1961, B 2/1961, and B 1/1962) contained requests for Council recommendations, following the standard formula used in member's proposals.

Four of the twenty-one governmental proposals represented a joint effort: Item A 31/1957 was introduced by the governments of Denmark, Norway, and Sweden; Items B 1/1961 and B 2/1961 were offered on behalf of the Nordic Ministerial Committee for Economic Cooperation; and Item B 3/1962, which proposed the Helsinki Agreement, was authored by all five governments. The remaining governmental proposals were presented by a single government, as follows: seven from Sweden, four from Finland, and three each from Denmark and Norway.

The elected members to the Nordic Council introduced 194 member's proposals during the years from 1953 to 1962. After rising to a record twenty-eight in 1958, the number of member's proposals offered at a single session leveled off to seventeen each at the 1960 and 1961 sessions, and then climbed again to twenty-six at the 1962 session (see chart 7).

The average number of authors for each bill has been about three and one half. Three-author proposals have been the most common, followed closely by one-author, two-author, and four-author measures. Nearly one fourth of all member's proposals have had five or more authors. Single-member authorship has been discouraged since 1955, when it burgeoned to include fifteen of the twenty-two member's proposals introduced that year. Swedish elected members were responsible for thirteen of the fifteen, and for twenty-four of an eight-year total of twenty-nine single-author proposals.

More than two thirds of member's proposals have authors from two or more countries. Here again, the single-nation author category was expanded by the unique surge of single-author bills in 1955. Single-nation member's proposals have also been on the decline since 1955. Excluding single-nation member's proposals, three-nation sponsorship has been the most popular. A comparison of member's proposals which have included an author or coauthor from a given country shows that Swedish authors have been by far the most active, followed by the roughly comparable efforts from those of Denmark, Norway, and Finland (in declining order), with Icelandic authors understandably lagging far behind.

The picture of Swedish predominance in the introduction of matters is even more striking in regard to languages used. The Statute and Rules of Procedure do not state which languages are permissible in the Council. By mutual agreement, however, only Danish, Norwegian, and Swedish have been used. Four times as many member's proposals have been written in Swedish as in Danish and Norwegian combined.

Swedish hegemony in the introduction of member's proposals coincides with a lesser Swedish predominance in the introduction of governmental proposals as already indicated. It is further consistent with the centralization of Nordic Council editorial and publishing activities in Stockholm, which was described in the preceding chapter.

In the first 8 years, only 11 of the 151 member's proposals were introduced by authors sharing the same political affiliation, but of differing nationalities. (Of these eleven, five had only two authors, and permit only a weak inference of cross-national party cohesion.) Nine member's proposals were introduced by authors of the same party and nationality. (Again, four of these were two-author bills.) The eleven cross-national proposals of uniform party origin contrast with the ninety-eight cross-national proposals in which party uniformity does not govern. However, the authors of thirteen of these ninety-eight matters present a spectrum of all the major parties, i.e., the Social Democrats, Liberals, Agrarians, and Conservatives. The desire for broad political representation shows an awareness of political affiliation, but is a negation of cross-national party cohesion. The joining together of all member's proposals in which authorship is correlated with political affiliation in one form or another gives a total of thirty-three, or about one fifth of all member's proposals. It follows that party membership is not a dominating force in bringing authors together, and that cross-national party cohesion in the introduction of proposals is slight. A somewhat higher correlation is found between coauthorship of a proposal and common membership on a Nordic Council organ. Moreover, this correlation is on the increase, while the party correlation has been somewhat declining.

Pursuant to Article IX of the Statute of the Nordic Council, only governments and individual elected members may introduce proposals in the Council. Joint authorship by elected members of the same committee, or by the members of the Presidium, is an effective way of providing for institutional authorship. Six proposals introduced by the members of the Presidium have had to do with the Statute or Rules of Procedure of the Council; in 1960, as an exception, the proposal for amendment of the Rules was introduced by members of the nine-man Interim Committee on Judiciary.

As far as committee bills are concerned, the great majority were introduced by members of the erstwhile interim committees. Excluding proposals with only one or two authors, the nine-man

Committees on Judiciary and Social Welfare each accounted for ten proposals to and including 1960, while the five standing committees accounted for only one proposal each.

Pursuant to Section 2(2) of the Rules of Procedure, deputy delegates may introduce matters if they are joined as coauthors by fully-elected members. About one fifth of all member's proposals have alternate members as coauthors. The reasons for coauthorship vary. In some cases, the deputy delegate may have belonged to an interim committee whose members were introducing a matter. In other cases, he may complete a desired spectrum of political or national sponsorship. Rarely, the alternate may be the principal author of a proposal, and the elected member merely a cooperative cosigner. Swedish deputy delegates have used this device more than those from all of the other countries combined; Icelanders have not used it at all.

Motions to amend governmental or member's proposals may be offered at any time before reference to committee, pursuant to Section 4 of the Rules of Procedure. They are usually presented on or before the day of the commencement of an annual session.

Governments have submitted amendatory proposals only three times—one Danish, one Norwegian, and one Swedish—in the ten years from 1953 to 1962. Elected members were responsible for twelve amendatory proposals during the same period (see chart 7), again with a marked predominance of Swedish authorship. The five members of the Presidium offered one amendatory proposal in 1959, following general debate on the breakdown of negotiations for a common Nordic market, and another in 1962, relating to the governments' proposal for the Helsinki Agreement.

Governmental Memoranda on Action Taken
Pursuant to Council Recommendation

Article XI of the Statute of the Nordic Council directs the governments to inform the Council at each ordinary session "of the action which has been taken on the recommendations of the Council." The governments have been faithful in submitting these memoranda: they did so each year from 1954 to 1959 with regard to every outstanding recommendation, except that in 1958 no memorandum was forthcoming on Recommendation 15/1954. However, this does not mean that each government submitted a memorandum on every outstanding recommendation, but only that one or

more governments did so. On the other hand, some of the memoranda carry several reports from the same country. The reports
range in size from a sentence or two to many pages, the latter
sometimes incorporating the reports of other organs of Scandinavian cooperation, which may, in turn, include the solicited views of
pertinent interest groups.

The Council did not comment on the single omission in 1958,
above, and it has not complained openly when less than all of the
governments submitted memoranda on a given matter—again with
a single exception. In considering the memorandum relating to
Recommendation 5/1958, the Standing Committee on Economic
Matters proposed that the reports of Denmark, Finland, Iceland,
and Norway be accepted, but noted that none "was as yet forthcoming from the coordinating country, i.e., Sweden." [2]

In the notice of impending session sent to the governments three
months before a session is to start, the Presidium indicates to the
governments which outstanding recommendations would be particularly appropriate for informative memoranda.

Pursuant to Section 3(1) of the Rules of Procedure, the memoranda are to be submitted "not later than one month before the
Session begins." The Presidium usually suggests that the memoranda be submitted an additional one or two weeks before this
deadline. Even as against the statutory deadline, the governments
have not been rigorously prompt. The least timely government has
submitted about one fifth of its memoranda less than one month
before the opening of a session. No dates were included in the
1954 memoranda, and their timeliness cannot be conveniently
determined. Moreover, the dates given in subsequent years are the
dates the memoranda were signed, which might precede the dates
of actual submission.

The governments of Denmark, Finland, Iceland, and Sweden
permit the ministries or departments to submit their reports directly to the Council. With a few exceptions in 1957, the government of Norway has required the operating agencies to transmit
their reports through the Norwegian Foreign Ministry.

As of 1961, there were 394 sets of memoranda, each with one or
more reports from one or more governments (see chart 8). The

[2] *Nordiska rådet: 7:e sessionen, 1959* ("The Nordic Council: Seventh
Session, 1959," hereinafter cited as *1959 Record;* the other annual records
will be similarly cited), p. 1994.

CHART 8.

NUMBER OF RECOMMENDATIONS ON WHICH MEMORANDA HAVE BEEN
SUBMITTED BY THE GOVERNMENTS, 1954–61

	Annual session in:								
	1954	1955	1956	1957	1958	1959	1960	1961	*Total*
Pertaining to recommendations made at annual session in:									
1953	11	6	6	4	2	2	0	2	33
1954		30	26	20	19	9	1	9	114
1955			16	15	9	5	0	5	50
1956				21	13	7	0	5	46
1957					27	14	4	9	54
1958						33	1	24	58
1959							3	24	27
1960								12	12
Total	11	36	48	60	70	70	9	90	394

rising number of outstanding recommendations has resulted in an
increasing number of memoranda to be submitted and considered
each year. There is a conscious effort to write off as many old
recommendations as possible, so that the number of memoranda
can be limited. In 1959, this policy resulted in a leveling of the
number of memoranda at 230, relating to 70 recommendations
(see chart 9). In spite of the clear directive of Article XI of the
Statute, the Presidium hinted to the governments that memoranda
need not be forthcoming at the 1960 session. Only nine were

CHART 9.

NUMBER OF NATIONAL CONTRIBUTIONS TO MEMORANDA, 1954–60

	Annual session in:							
	1954	1955	1956	1957	1958	1959	1960	*Total*
Denmark	9	34	44	43	53	47	6	236
Finland	x	x	x	32	50	56	6	144
Iceland	1	4	14	0	11	11	5	46
Norway	9	30	40	45	54	54	7	239
Sweden	9	35	44	57	59	62	7	273
Total	28	103	142	177	227	230	31	938

x = Finland not yet participating

submitted. Memoranda were again submitted on ninety recommendations at the 1961 session, however, and on eighty-six at the 1962 session. The Presidium presented a list of ninety-six outstanding recommendations on which it was awaiting governmental memoranda at the 1963 session. In 1964 and 1965, the number rose to 98 and 102, respectively.

Since 1957, some memoranda have been accepted without reference to committee and without substantial consideration by the Council in plenary session, pursuant to Section 12(1) of the Rules of Procedure. The Presidium and Joint Working Committee select those memoranda which seem to require no current action by the Council, and move that they be accepted without committee action, usually awaiting a new memorandum the following year. Memoranda relating to seventeen recommendations were summarily treated in 1957, as were those relating to fifteen recommendations in 1958, thirty-one in 1959, forty-three—nearly half—in 1961, and twenty-six in 1962.

Reports on Scandinavian Cooperation

The Statute of the Nordic Council makes no reference to reports on Scandinavian cooperation. Section 2(1) of the Rules of Procedure of the Council states that a matter may be introduced as a member's proposal or a governmental proposal, or "by a memorandum of the type referred to in Article XI of the Statute, or by a report on Scandinavian cooperation." Section 3(1) of the Rules requires that such reports "be submitted to a secretariat not later than one month before the session begins." The reports have generally been timely, although the partial or entire absence of dates in a number of them prevents a convenient determination of their promptness. A few reports have been clearly late—three in 1953, one in 1954, one in 1959—but this has not prevented their being considered by the Council.

In a letter preceding the three months' notice of impending session, the Presidium tells the governments which reports it would like to have and suggests topics for special emphasis. This coordination has a dual aspect: it is designed to ensure the submission of suitable reports, and also to prevent the production of unwanted reports. In the absence of such communication, the governments submitted eight reports at the first annual session which the Council did not even bother to print! The reports were accepted on first reading, without debate and without reference to committee.

Reports on Scandinavian cooperation have been of two main types. The so-called permanent organs of cooperation (described in the next chapter) report regularly to the Council on their activities, and the governments submit reports on special problems or areas of cooperation, as requested by the Presidium. In the ten years from 1953 to 1962, there were fifty-three of the former and twenty-eight of the latter.

Subject matter reports were especially prominent at the first annual session in 1953, when reports were submitted on the history of postwar cooperation in the fields of social welfare, commerce, cultural affairs, and uniform laws. Other such reports have dealt with more specific topics, such as Nordic television, research on infantile paralysis, and Arctic roads.

Except for the year 1960, when the Council did not request them, there have been from five to twelve reports on Scandinavian cooperation submitted each year (see chart 7). They are usually submitted through the government of the host country of a given session. Sometimes, however, the same government has repeatedly forwarded a particular report to the Council.

In 1953 and 1954, some of the administrative organs of cooperation sent their reports directly to the Council. This was the procedure suggested by the head of the Danish delegation, President Hans Hedtoft. However, Foreign Minister Halvard Lange of Norway and Foreign Minister Östen Undén of Sweden felt that the reports should be submitted through a government. The Norwegian and Swedish members of the Presidium agreed that this would be the best procedure to follow. Two organs sent their reports directly in 1954, but since 1955, all reports have been transmitted through a government. In one case, the same report was submitted by two governments, and in another case, three governments presented a joint report on economic cooperation. In forwarding a report on Scandinavian cooperation, the governments do not necessarily endorse the proposals contained in it.

In 1959, the Danish government forwarded a report from the Consultative Committee on Questions of Atomic Energy which stated that there was "no occasion for the preparation of a full report on the work of the past year." [3] The Presidium decided

[3] *1959 Record,* p. 1271.

to challenge this unilateral determination, and the Norwegian member of the Presidium called attention to it in plenary session, with a request for a full report in subsequent years. The Swedish Minister of Commerce, Gunnar Lange, replied testily that the Council's wishes would be respected.[4] The duty of the permanent organs of cooperation to report annually has been established, even in the absence of statutory requirement.

Supplementary Proposals

Section 4 of the Rules of Procedure of the Nordic Council states that "In connection with a memorandum or a report, proposals (supplementary proposals) may be submitted . . . not later than seven days before a session begins." Almost all supplementary proposals have been timely. Sixty were offered during the first ten years of the Council. Only two of the sixty had governmental authorship. In recent years, supplementary proposals have been attached to memoranda, but not to reports. At the 1962 session, there was a remarkable upsurge of supplementary proposals, twenty in all, or half as many as had been introduced throughout the preceding nine years. Consequently, there were more proposals to consider at the 1962 session than at any previous one (see chart 7).

Swedish elected members have been the most active in offering supplementary proposals, just as they were with member's proposals and amendatory proposals. From 1953 to 1961 Swedes were authors or coauthors of twenty-seven out of thirty-nine member's supplementary proposals, including twelve out of twenty single-author bills. Three fourths of the supplementary proposals were written in the Swedish language.

The pattern of authorship of supplementary proposals is consistent with that of authorship of member's proposals in general. There is little party cohesion, and a somewhat greater tendency to seek broad national, as opposed to broad political, authorship. The authors of a few member's supplementary proposals have been united by common membership in a Nordic Council organ.

Reports from the Presidium of the Nordic Council

The first Presidium report, in 1954, took up only one page, although it was supplemented with an oral summary of interim

[4] *Ibid.,* pp. 105–6.

activities by the Swedish Vice-President, Nils Herlitz. In 1955, the report of the Presidium took the form which it has since retained. It included sections on the composition and meetings of the Presidium, on steps taken pursuant to outstanding Council recommendations, on participation of Council representatives in meetings of Nordic ministers, on preparations for the upcoming session, on "other matters" (including communications from pressure groups), and on the national delegations and their relations with the home parliaments.

In 1956, a new category was added to the report, covering financial matters. Two miscellaneous matters were included in the body of the report in 1956, and one was added as an appendix. The use of appendices became standard for miscellaneous matters starting in 1957, while the body of the report retained its previous form. Miscellaneous matters have included such diverse topics as the procedures and effectiveness of the Council, exchange of civil servants between the countries, problems of Lapland, and so forth.

In 1958, as a result of their increasing numbers, incoming communications were taken from the section on "other matters" and made into a separate section. The Presidium receives about a score a year. Communications have been received from individuals and from private and semipublic organizations with complaints or suggestions on matters such as double taxation or employment rights in neighboring countries. More recently, the Presidium has referred these communications to the appropriate Nordic Council standing committee.

The 1958 report of the Presidium contained two communications from the Presidium to the governments, the first recorded instances of this method of calling governmental attention to specific problems of cooperation. Presidential communications are tantamount to recommendations.[5] At the same time, the Presidium hopes to forestall member's proposals which might otherwise be directed to these problems. One of the 1958 letters concerned the right of ministers to conduct marriages for seamen of their own nationality in a neighboring Nordic country, while the other related to the mutual transference of wife or child support payments.

[5] Such is the assertion of the Council secretariat in Gustaf Petrén (ed.), *Nordiska rådets verksamhet 1952–1961* (Stockholm: Nordisk udrednings-serie, No. 8, 1962), p. 11. See also *Översikt över lagar tillkomna genom nordiskt samarbete* (Stockholm: Nordisk udredningsserie, No. 2, 1965).

The 1959 Presidium report followed earlier patterns, including successive innovations, and added to the appendices a communication from the government of Denmark to the Nordic Council. The report of the Presidium at the 1960 session was one of the few matters not greatly foreshortened for that brief meeting. No new categories were added in 1960, 1961, and 1962, but the previous ones were used. The 1959, 1960, and 1962 reports each included three communications from the Presidium to the governments.

The committees also submit reports on their interim activities, listing the names of their members, officers, and staff, and giving a chronology of activities (see chart 7). With the disappearance of separate interim committees, the reports of the standing committees are simply included in the report of the Presidium.

Matters Postponed from a Previous Session

There is no express authorization in the Statute of the Nordic Council for postponing a matter to a subsequent session. However, the power to do so is clearly within the scope of the Article XII direction that the "Council shall adopt its own Rules of Procedure."

Section 12(3) of the Rules of Procedure of the Council states that a "given matter shall be decided upon at the meeting for which the standing committee's proposal has been placed on the agenda, unless the Council decides to postpone it to a later meeting or to a later session." Deferment to a later session is also referred to in Sections 1, 4, and 9 of the Rules.

An initial postponement has been suggested by the Swedish secretariat as the best method for treating many new member's proposals, as follows:

> The majority of new Member's Proposals [should receive] a pre-liminary consideration which aims at determining if the question merits further deliberation at all. . . . If the Proposal is not directly rejected by the Council, it ought to be postponed to the following Session. The interval should be used for further investigation of the matter.[6]

During the first eight sessions, there were fifty-one postponements, relating to thirty-six items. Twenty-six of these were single post-

[6] *1958 Record,* p. 1635.

ponements, while there were six double postponements, three triple postponements, and one instance in which a decreasing portion of a matter was successively postponed four times. Thirteen items were postponed at the 1961 session, as were fifteen at the 1962 session, including eight of that year's supplementary proposals.

Preparing the Agenda

There are two agendas at each session, one for the entire session, called the sessional agenda, and the other for a single meeting within a session. The latter is governed by Section 11(2) of the Rules of Procedure, which directs the Presidium to prepare an agenda for each meeting, "Giving regard to whatever the Council may have decided on the consideration of matters." The outgoing Presidium prepares the agenda for the first meeting of a session. Each daily agenda makes up part of the sessional agenda.

In accordance with Section 9 of the Rules of Procedure, the Council adopts a sessional agenda at the first meeting of a session. This agenda includes all matters raised under the provisions of Section 3 of the Rules of Procedure—member's proposals, governmental proposals, memoranda on action taken on Council recommendations, and reports on Scandinavian cooperation. Although not specifically mentioned in either Section 9 or Section 11, amendatory proposals and supplementary proposals are included as part of the primary subject matter to which they relate. Reports of the Presidium and of the committees are included in the appropriate daily agenda, but not in the sessional agenda (see chart 7).

In 1956, code letters were added to the number assigned to each item, as follows: "A" to indicate that the matter is a member's proposal or a governmental proposal (but see below); "B" to designate a report from a Council organ, such as the Presidium or an interim committee (but see below); "C" to signify that the matter is a report on Scandinavian cooperation; and "D" to mean that the matter is a governmental memorandum on action taken on a Council recommendation. In 1958, the letter "B" was taken away from internal Council reports, which now have no code designation, and was given to governmental proposals. The letter "A" has since been used exclusively for member's proposals. Starting at the 1965 session, lower-case letters were added to designate the standing committee to which the matter had been referred, as follows: "e," Economic Matters; "j," Judiciary; "k," Cultural Affairs; "s," Social Policy; and "t," Communications (literally, "Traffic").

The first act of the Council-in-session is to approve the roster of members, as prepared by the Chief Clerk pursuant to Section 6(1) of the Rules of Procedure. No seat has ever been contested, and no procedure is specified for testing the credentials of members designate.

The elected members and the governmental representatives are seated separately, each in alphabetical order, without regard to nationality or political affiliation. At the 1961 session, the cabinet members were merged with the ordinary members, but the old system was restored in 1962.

After the roster has been approved, the new Presidium is elected. Next, the Council approves the sessional agenda and sets up the standing committees.

After disposing of these formalities, the members turn to general debate. These debates have been characterized by a certain artificiality, although the 1959 exchanges on the reasons for the breakdown of negotiations for a common Nordic market were seemingly spontaneous. The Presidium, aided by the Secretaries-General, organizes the debate and decides what the topics should be. The theme is introduced in the welcoming addresses of the outgoing and incoming Presidents.

In 1953 and 1954, there was general debate on the motion for adoption or amendment of the Rules of Procedure. In 1955, President Nils Herlitz informed the Council that the general debate would deal with "the Council and its tasks." [7] Similarly, in 1956, President Erik Eriksen stated that the topic for general debate would be "the Council, its procedures and its tasks, and Nordic cooperation in general." [8]

The subject for general debate was not defined beforehand in 1957 and 1958, although in the latter year it was made clear that the debate on economic cooperation was to take place in connection with the consideration of the memorandum on Recommendation 22/1954, which related directly to that subject.

In 1959, the Speaker noted that there were no special restric-

[7] *1955 Record*, p. 35.
[8] *1956 Record*, p. 50.

tions on general debate. Some of the elected members took the governments to task for not having carried through a common Nordic market before entering the newly established European Free Trade Association. As an innovation, since retained, short replies were permitted, and the exchanges were lively.

The 1960 general debate treated again with Council purposes and procedures, especially with the relationship between the Council and the governments. One topic—research and higher education—was reserved for later consideration, at the request of the Joint Working Committee.

The Presidium suggested four topics for general debate in 1961, and instructed those who wished to treat with more than one of them to take the floor separately for each subject. Sporadic jumping from one issue to another was thus avoided. The four themes were the Nordic Council and Nordic cooperation—the perennial basis for general debate—the Nordic implications of European economic integration, problems of coordination in higher education and research, and aid to underdeveloped countries.

The anniversary represented by the tenth annual session of the Nordic Council in 1962 provided the occasion for another examination of the history and portent of Nordic cooperation, as did the topic of regional confrontation—between and among the members of EEC, EFTA, and GATT (General Agreement on Tariffs and Trade)—which has dominated general debate at all subsequent sessions.

In 1953 and 1954, one or two members of the Presidium opened the debate. From 1955 to 1958, the first speakers were Prime Ministers. Since 1959, there has been greater alternation between members of the Presidium, cabinet members, and ordinary elected members. Not until the debates on economic cooperation was the Council able to inspire any more than a routine participation on the part of cabinet members. The words of Einar Gerhardsen, then Prime Minister of Norway and a charter Vice-President of the Council, are revealing on this point:

> It is hardly a secret to some that especially the so-called general debates are arranged, as from time to time it is necessary to do, and that it is not the Governments who arrange the debates, but it is the Nordic Council's leadership, its Presidium and its secretariat. I have heard before that there has been expression of displeasure over [the fact that] in previous debates the Prime Ministers have stood up in

turn as the first on the list of speakers and made their contribution to the debate. So that no one will misunderstand this, I would like to make the observation that, as far as I know, the Prime Ministers have never requested this. It has in fact been in response to the wish of the Nordic Council's leadership that one took the floor so early in debate and gave expression to particular opinions. But from the Governments' side, this is not a satisfactory arrangement, and I want to commend the Presidium on the practice it has now hit upon with the Presidium's own members in the first instance opening the debate and thus providing an interplay on which both the other members of the Council and the Governmental members have some natural basis for exchanging words.[9]

The Norwegian delegation to the Nordic Council has been the most active in general debate. Norwegian elected members have spoken more than twice as often as those of any other country (see chart 10). In the period from 1953 to 1960, no general debate transpired without some expression of opinion from the representatives of the Norwegian Labor and Conservative parties, while the Liberals failed to participate only in 1959. A Christian People's party delegate has joined in debate every year since 1955.

The reason for this activity is found in the Norwegian bourgeois parties' opposition to the Council, first evident when the Council was being formed. The Conservative, Christian People's, and Center parties have been the most consistent and outspoken opponents of Nordic bureaucracy. They would like to cut down on the amount of paper used by the Council, and some of them would prefer to see the Council meet only every other year. The attitude of the Norwegian Liberal party has been mixed, while the Social Democrats have met bourgeois arguments with weak rebuttal, cautioning the Council against overextending itself.

Norwegian participation in general debate declined in 1959, in spite of the extensiveness of that debate, which was the longest in Council history. Many of the other members of the Council were disappointed over the abandonment of the proposed common Nordic market, while the Norwegian opposition parties had feared the contrary. Instead of attacking the Council for its failure, the Norwegian opposition offered the solace that there were other meaningful areas of cooperation to which the Council could make a significant contribution.

The passing of the common Nordic market issue has left the

9 *1960 Record*, pp. 53–54.

CHART 10.

PARTICIPATION IN GENERAL DEBATE AT EACH ANNUAL SESSION, 1953–62

Members from:	1953	1954	1955	1956	1957	1958	1959	1960	1961	1962	*Total*
Denmark											
Elected	1	2	2	1	3	1	3	3	7	5	28
Ministerial	0	1	1	1	1	1	2	1	3	3	14
Total	1	3	3	2	4	2	5	4	10	8	42
Finland											
Elected	x	x	x	2	1	1	5	2	2	2	15
Ministerial	x	x	x	1	1	1	2	1	2	1	9
Total				3	2	2	7	3	4	3	24
Iceland											
Elected	1	0	1	0	1	1	0	0	0	2	6
Ministerial	0	0	–	1	–	–	–	2	1	1	5
Total	1	0	1	1	1	1	0	2	1	3	11
Norway											
Elected	6	3	5	7	6	5	4	6	6	5	53
Ministerial	1	1	1	1	1	1	1	2	2	3	14
Total	7	4	6	8	7	6	5	8	8	8	67
Sweden											
Elected	4	3	3	2	1	1	1	3	3	4	25
Ministerial	1	1	1	1	1	1	2	2	4	2	16
Total	5	4	4	3	2	2	3	5	7	6	41
Total											
Elected	12	8	11	12	12	9	13	14	18	18	127
Ministerial	2	3	3	5	4	4	7	8	12	10	58
Total	14	11	14	17	16	13	20	22	30	28	185

x = Finland not yet a member

– = No Icelandic cabinet members in attendance

Council without a major controversial topic for debate, the concern over which is heightened by the fact that debate in plenary session is often televised regionally through the Nordvision network. The procedures of the Council remain a target for occasional carping comment, but for the most part there is no venting of difference of opinion. So little else presents itself that the absence of controversy becomes contentious. The Norwegian Liberal, Helge Seip, gave pointed expression to this condition in the 1960 general debate:

Mr. President. As I sat and listened to the debate this morning, it struck me that we were so much in agreement that I would say there was a distastefully strong unanimity present. There was unanimity to such a degree that one asked himself involuntarily if the Nordic Council in reality was not in a very serious situation, in a crisis in the sense that we are about to drown the whole Council in our unanimity—in a unanimity which easily becomes sterile, because there must always be conformity among us on all points.[10]

When the general debate is concluded, the Council accepts the report of the Presidium and proceeds to first reading of the items on the agenda.

FIRST READING: REFERENCE TO COMMITTEE

Section 12(1) of the Rules of Procedure of the Nordic Council provides that the "Council shall refer the matters included in the agenda to standing committees as soon as possible. . . . However, a matter may be decided without reference to committee by unanimous decision of the Council." The latter provision was used in 1953 and again every year since 1957 to except some reports, memoranda, or member's proposals from committee consideration. Through 1962, 8 reports, 132 memoranda, and 13 member's proposals received this summary treatment.

Section 12(4) of the Rules further relaxes compulsory reference to committee by providing that "Questions which relate only to the internal workings of the Council may be decided upon without reference to committee." Thus, reports of the Presidium are not sent to committee.

Except as noted above, all matters before the Council are referred to standing committee. The standing committees do not vie for bills, but permit the Presidium and secretariat to effect a rough numerical equality in the assignment of proposals, memoranda, and reports. The Standing Committee on Economic Matters has been seized with fewer items than the other committees—although the difference is not overwhelming—but it has deliberated on the most weighty single matter to come before the Council, the proposed common Nordic market. In a few cases, the appropriate committee for a given matter has been in doubt. In resolving the doubt, the Chief Clerk acts as parliamentarian and advises the Speaker. It is typical of the spirit of compromise which permeates

[10] *Ibid.*, p. 67.

the Council to send borderline matters to more than one committee, either formally or informally.

Section 12(1) of the Rules also establishes the right of members to comment on matters being referred to committee. In 1953 and 1954, the general debate itself was on the motion to refer the proposed Rules of Procedure to the Standing Committee on Judiciary. However, the Presidium has consistently discouraged extensive use of debate on first reading. In 1956, 1957, and 1958, the presiding officer informed the Council that comments accompanying reference to committee were not intended to be genuine debate, such as that which was expected on second reading. Nevertheless, certain matters have been debated on first reading, particularly those relating to economic cooperation in 1953, 1956, and 1958. Otherwise, comments at this stage have been brief and rare, and debate on first reading has been almost completely dispensed with since 1959.

Reference to committee has become increasingly routine. In 1953 and 1954, all matters going to the same committee were taken in turn, while from 1955 to 1958 matters were taken in their numerical order, regardless of the committee to which they were to be sent. The practice of reading only the number of a matter and not its title was tried in 1958 by Vice-President Nils Hønsvald of Norway. The *coup de grâce* was delivered in 1959, when matters were referred to committee en masse, by adoption of a blanket proposal. Since the end of the 1964 session, the Presidium has authorized the secretariat to refer matters to the standing committees immediately upon their introduction, which is to say, during the interim between sessions.

DELIBERATIONS OF THE STANDING COMMITTEES

Paragraph 1 of the Directions for Committee Work provides that the "first meeting of the committee shall be brought to order by the member whose name stands first on the alphabetically prepared list of members elected to the committee." The Presidium sets the time for the opening meeting, which takes place following the first plenary meeting of the session. In addition to the opening meeting, each standing committee usually holds two half-day meetings during the day set aside for them, and one or two meetings during the closing days of the session.

The first act of each standing committee is to elect its chairman and vice-chairman, pursuant to Paragraph 1(a) of the Directions for Committee Work. (Actually, the officers are chosen by the Presidium or the Joint Working Committee, and this choice is ratified by the committee.) Next, the chairman introduces the committee secretary, already chosen by the Presidium and announced in plenary session. Third, each committee confirms the right of certain nonmembers to attend meetings, as described in the following paragraphs.

Section 13(2) of the Rules of Procedure of the Council authorizes the standing committees to invite elected members from other committees and cabinet members who are not ministerial representatives to the Council to attend committee hearings, and to "otherwise invite persons outside the Council to give information or make statements. . . ."

Paragraphs 1(c), 1(d), and 1(e) of the Directions for Committee Work instruct the standing committees to invite ministerial representatives, elected members from other committees, deputy delegates, and experts to attend committee hearings. The ministerial representatives are to "participate," the elected members and deputies are to "attend," and the experts are to "assist." In practice, few members of other committees or alternates attend, ministerial representatives do not always participate actively in discussions, and the experts often do more than merely assist the committees.

The members of the Presidium and the Secretaries-General are entitled to attend committee meetings and to take the floor without special invitation, pursuant to Paragraph 3 of the Directions for Committee Work. The committee secretary is also included in the Paragraph 3 authorization to join in committee discussions.

Except for those to deputy delegates and experts, the invitations are extended in blanket fashion, and the standing committees have little discretion in excluding any who belong to these privileged groups.

Moreover, the committees are equally restricted in deciding whom to invite in addition to those who must be invited. The Presidium prepares a list of experts, in the confident hope that the committees will not go outside the list in inviting specialists and civil servants. The committees are reminded of this list in Paragraph 1(e) of the Directions. More emphatically, Paragraph 2, added in 1959, states that "Deliberations of the committees are closed, and the committee should not make its meetings public."

Committee hearings, then, are not considered as part of the "deliberations of the Council" which, according to Article VI of the Statute, "shall be public." The clear policy against open committee meetings developed in response to the attempts of the young people's auxiliaries of the various political parties to secure admission to committee hearings.

The committees have also seen their independence circumscribed in another way, implied in their request to the Presidium to instruct the experts to leave the committee room after they have testified. The Presidium took cognizance of this problem in 1958, but responded in 1959 by adding a mere permissive sentence to Paragraph 3 of the Directions, which indicated that each standing committee must decide for itself whether the experts should be excluded "at the moment when decisions are reached." This sentence was deleted in 1961. The problem was stated in the 1958 report of the Presidium as follows:

> Sometimes it happens that the experts also see it to be their duty . . . to try to induce the committee to reach a decision in conformity with the particular department's or ministry's or agency's desires. It has become a problem in the work of the Council to determine just how expertise of this kind can be used without the committee members being unduly influenced in making their decisions. Perhaps their presence in committee should be limited to the stage of introductory discussion. However, precise rules in such a matter would be hard to formulate.[11]

The reason for the diffidence displayed in this last sentence and in the short-lived amendment to Paragraph 3 of the Directions is that the elected members often desire to delegate decision-making power to the experts, and to rely on the experts to formulate the particular language of the committee proposal.

Having acknowledged the choice of its officers and its secretary, and having ratified the invitations for others to attend, the committee proceeds to follow the instructions of Paragraph 1(f) of the Directions for Committee Work that "it establish a preliminary

---

[11] *1958 Record,* pp. 1633–34. According to Einar Løchen, "Arbeidsformene i Nordisk Råd og Europarådet," *Nordisk Kontakt,* No. 8 (1963), p. 440: ". . . it may be that the Cabinet Members and the experts in some cases have exerted such a great influence that proposals have been watered down or that, in a controversial matter, no recommendation has been adopted at all."

program for its work." Until 1965, discretion was limited by the circumstance that each committee had to consider and report back on all matters referred to it.

The committee secretary keeps the minutes of the meetings. Paragraph 4 of the Directions instructs him to record the time of opening and closing of each meeting, the names of those in attendance, and "the decisions reached by the committee." The elected members have been conscientious in attending committee meetings. All of the committee members are usually present, although one or two may be absent from time to time. The presence of members from other standing committees, or of alternate delegates, or of members of Parliament not elected to the Council, or of cabinet members not appointed as ministerial representatives, has been rare. The Secretaries-General of the national delegations attend committee hearings occasionally.

Ministerial representatives have been present for the deliberations of about three quarters of the matters before committee. Usually, there are only one or two cabinet members present, but the number reaches six or seven on occasion, and once reached a total of thirteen ministers in regard to Economic Matters Committee Proposal 9/1958, which dealt with the proposed common Nordic market.

Ministerial representatives have been present for the consideration of roughly 50 per cent of the deliberations of the Standing Committee on Communications, 60 per cent of those of the Standing Committee on Cultural Affairs, 70 per cent of those of the Standing Committee on Social Policy, 85 per cent of those of the Standing Committee on Judiciary, and 90 per cent of those of the Standing Committee on Economic Matters. These percentages are an approximate measure of the relative importance the ministers attach to the several committees.

The over-all rate of committee attendance by experts is slightly lower than that for ministerial representatives. The committee with the lowest rate of ministerial attendance has been the one with the highest proportion of assistance from civil servants: expert witnesses were present for the consideration of 90 per cent of the proposals made by the Standing Committee on Communications. The Standing Committee on Social Policy is in the middle of both scales: experts were present for the consideration of 80 per cent of the Social Policy proposals. The remaining three committees—

Cultural Affairs, Judiciary, and Economic Matters—all had rates of participation of experts of about 50 per cent. The latter two committees had the highest rates of ministerial attention, while the Cultural Affairs Committee was relatively neglected in both categories—perhaps because it was overshadowed by the Nordic Cultural Commission.

Paragraph 5 of the Directions for Committee Work states that "Each matter shall be laid before the committee by a committee member, the committee secretary, or a summoned expert." The 1958 report of the Presidium indicates that a "matter is presented in committee by a civil servant, preferably the Council's own, [and one] who is not already engaged to represent the views of some other organ." [12] The committee may be offered a proposed draft for its report at this time.

Until 1964, the documents before the committee on a given matter included the report of the interim committee, if any. The interim committees made individual recommendations on seven matters before the 1957 session, seventeen each at the 1958 and 1959 sessions, twelve at the 1960 session, fourteen at the 1961 session, twenty-two at the 1962 session, and thirty-one at the 1963 session. In almost every case, the action of the standing committee was consistent with the views expressed by the interim committee, and where specific proposals were made, the standing committee adopted them, usually in the precise language used by the interim committee.

After the introductory presentation, the experts express their views and respond to questions. Next, the committee members discuss the matter informally and arrive at a decision. Voting is by simple majority. One half of the members constitute a quorum, pursuant to Section 18 of the Rules of Procedure. Section 13(4) of the Rules gives the committee chairman the tie-breaking vote.

Section 13(1) of the Rules of Procedure and Paragraph 6 of the Directions for Committee Work empower, but do not require, each committee to appoint a spokesman, or *rapporteur,* to present the committee's views on a given matter in plenary session. Spokesmen have almost invariably been appointed for each matter.

Section 13(4) of the Rules establishes the right of "Any member of a standing committee . . . to submit a proposal which differs from that submitted by the committee." And, according to

[12] *1958 Record,* p. 1634.

Section 13(1) of the Rules, a "minority of a standing committee may also elect a spokesman." The minority proposals are included in the committee proposals as reservations, pursuant to Paragraph 7 of the Directions for Committee Work.

Finally, the committee must approve the formulation which has been given the proposal. Paragraph 7 of the Directions specifies that the committee proposal

> . . . shall contain information as to who has participated in or been present at the consideration of a matter in committee, reference to documents and other papers which have been before the committee, the basis for the decision of the committee, the decision itself, and any reservations (minority proposals). The proposal shall be formulated in the language of the person who has drafted it.

Usually the committee secretary drafts the committee proposal, and, as indicated above, his language is used. In formulating the proposal, he may have worked with the original author of the proposal, with the spokesman appointed by the committee, with a drafting subcommittee appointed by the committee, with an expert in the field, with the Secretaries-General, or with some combination of these. The Chief Clerk examines the committee proposal to ensure its technical adequacy.

Committee proposals emerge from committees in direct proportion to the number of matters referred to them (see chart 11).

CHART 11.

COMMITTEE PROPOSALS, 1953–62

Standing Committee on:	Annual session in:										*Total*
	1953	1954	1955	1956	1957	1958	1959	1960	1961	1962	
Cultural Affairs	3	10	13	15	17	18	13	8	16	22	135
Economic Matters	5	8	14	6	11	11	11	4	16	19	105
Communications	x	x	x	19	19	21	14	4	13	18	108
Social Policy	3	15	20	20	12	22	17	6	9	19	143
Judiciary	3	17	14	17	14	21	14	6	15	19	140
Total	14	50	61	77	73	93	69	28	69	97	631

x = Communications separated from Economic Matters in 1956

There are fewer proposals than matters referred, since several of the latter may be disposed of in a single committee proposal.

The operative part of a committee proposal is the decision. Previous proposals—governmental, member's, amendatory, supplementary—are merged in the decision, and it is the decision, together with minority proposals, on which the Council will vote in plenary session. Thus, Section 15(1) of the Rules of Procedure notes that the consent of the Council is "required when, in the course of Council debate, a member presents a proposal for a recommendation which is not occasioned by the report of a standing committee."

In their treatment of matters which contain an initial proposal of one kind or another, the committees are asked by Paragraph 8 of the Directions for Committee Work to phrase their decisions in terms of "the adoption of a recommendation, a rejection (take no action), or postponement." As for memoranda on action taken on Council recommendations and reports on Scandinavian cooperation, Paragraph 8 notes that it "is assumed that [they] will be accepted." Without exception, they have been. In the case of memoranda, however, the committees are also directed to indicate "whether a new memorandum is awaited at a later session."

It was established at the first annual session that the standing committees could use reports and memoranda as a basis for recommendations to the governments, even when they are not accompanied by supplementary proposals on reference to committee. In recent years, however, the standing committees have not availed themselves of this opportunity and have merely proposed acceptance of the reports and memoranda.

The absence of dissent in committee has been most striking. Out of 534 committee proposals in 9 years, there were only 15 reservations, or less than 3 per cent. Four of these were submitted by a single dissenter, while eight were offered jointly by two dissenters, two by three dissenters, and one by four dissenters. The Judiciary Committee has experienced a few more minority reports than the others, followed in frequency by the Standing Committees on Social Policy, Economic Matters, Cultural Affairs, and Communications, respectively. The last committee did not see the expression of a single dissent during the first seven years of its existence.

Unanimity is attained by accepting those views which favor the least positive action. Thus, with rare exception, every member has a veto right over an affirmative decision. Anders Pettersson, a Swedish Agrarian and charter elected member to the Council, made the following remarks about the nature of the committee consideration given his proposal by the Standing Committee on Social Policy:

> . . . In a Swedish parliamentary committee . . . the majority actually dictates the report which is to be presented to the Parliament. In the Council's Social Policy committee one can say that it is practically the opposite. . . . [T]he most negative part of the committee is that which in reality dictates the Decision.[13]

While the formal rules require only a simple majority for a positive recommendation, the actual practice is to require unanimity or near unanimity. This convergence of views, at whatever level it occurs, is first measured in committee. It is then continued by the Council in plenary session. No committee proposal has ever been rejected by the Council. Only a few technical, corrective amendments have been adopted on the floor, in all of which the committee itself has concurred.

The leaders of the Nordic Council recognize and are concerned with the artificiality of the agreement displayed in many committee proposals. In the 1958 report of the Presidium, it was stated that "A further goal is that committee work [avoid] fictive unity. Where there are inconsistent views, it is better to report them. The committee members ought to be ready to defend the different approaches in . . . plenary session."[14] This goal has not been attained.

SECOND READING: DEBATE AND FINAL DISPOSITION

Debate

As the standing committees complete their deliberations on particular matters, they send their reports back to the floor. Section 12(2) of the Rules of Procedure provides that a "matter which has been considered by a standing committee may first be taken up for decision on the second day after the committee proposal has been received by the Council. The Council may, however, decide that the matter shall be considered sooner." In practice, a blanket

[13] *1957 Record*, p. 141.
[14] *1958 Record*, p. 1624.

waiver of the two-day delay has been granted whenever requested by the presiding officer, to permit the Council to consider committee proposals received the previous day.

Pursuant to Section 14(1) of the Rules of Procedure of the Council, members—whether elected or ministerial—may "speak in the order in which they have asked for the floor." Thus, the committee spokesman is not always the first to speak on the committee proposal for which he is responsible. Section 14(1) also provides that the "presiding officer may deviate from this order, subject to the approval of the Council." Section 7(2) of the Rules keeps the speaker from participating in debate. The standing committees are urged by Paragraph 6 of the Directions for Committee Work to prepare a list of speakers for debate in "questions of greater import," but they have not done so.

A large number of matters is debated, and a high proportion of members participate in debate (see charts 12A and 13). Many of

CHART 12.

NUMBER OF MATTERS DEBATED ON SECOND READING, 1953–62

Annual session in:

	1953	1954	1955	1956	1957	1958	1959	1960	1961	1962
A	10	40	36	38	53	46	47	18	52	38
B	8	13	15	14	22	14	17	8	25	13
C	2	1	1	2	3	1	5	0	5	5

A. Total number of matters debated
B. Number of matters debated by others than standing committee spokesman
C. Number of matters debated in which ministerial representatives joined in debate

these matters, however, are given a perfunctory introduction by the committee spokesman. The number of matters seriously debated is much smaller (see chart 12B). The contributions of ministerial representatives to debate on second reading are even more modest (see charts 12C and 13).

Efforts to make debate less desultory have been of no avail. Cabinet members have not acceded to requests that they participate more frequently. Nor does it seem likely that they will. Thus, for example, the then Finnish Minister of Agriculture, Johannes Virolainen—later Prime Minister, and, in 1959, vice-chairman of the Finnish Nordic Council national delegation—stated emphati-

CHART 13.

PARTICIPATION IN DEBATE ON SECOND READING, 1953–62

Members from:	Annual session in: 1953	1954	1955	1956	1957	1958	1959	1960	1961	1962	*Total*
Denmark:											
Elected	13	13	11	11	12	10	11	7	10	9	107
Ministerial	1	1	0	2	2	1	2	0	4	1	14
Total	14	14	11	13	14	11	13	7	14	10	121
Finland:											
Elected	x	x	x	1	11	9	10	6	10	7	54
Ministerial	x	x	x	1	1	1	1	0	2	2	8
Total				2	12	10	11	6	12	9	62
Iceland:											
Elected	2	2	4	2	2	3	2	2	2	1	22
Ministerial	0	0	—	0	—	—	—	0	0	1	1
Total	2	2	4	2	2	3	2	2	2	2	23
Norway:											
Elected	12	14	10	16	15	14	11	6	11	14	123
Ministerial	0	1	0	1	2	1	3	0	1	1	10
Total	12	15	10	17	17	15	14	6	12	15	133
Sweden:											
Elected	14	14	14	10	11	13	13	5	10	12	116
Ministerial	1	1	1	2	2	1	0	0	2	2	12
Total	15	15	15	12	13	14	13	5	12	14	128
Total:											
Elected	41	43	39	40	51	49	47	26	43	43	422
Ministerial	2	3	1	6	7	4	6	0	9	7	45
Total	43	46	40	46	58	53	53	26	52	50	467

x = Finland not yet a member
— = No Icelandic cabinet members in attendance

cally in general debate at the 1962 session that the governments ought to listen and learn at the annual sessions, but should not otherwise take too active a part in them.[15]

Section 14(2) of the Rules permits cloture of debate by a two-thirds vote on the nondebatable motion of the presiding officer or five elected members. This provision has never been used, although the presiding officer has occasionally requested the speakers to be brief.

[15] *1962 Record*, p. 51.

Voting

Article III of the Statute of the Nordic Council provides that the "ministerial representatives have no vote in the Council." The voting members are those elected by the five parliaments. One half of the voting members constitute a quorum, pursuant to Section 18 of the Rules of Procedure. While there is no provision for a call of the house, a recommendation would not be valid if it did not show on its face the presence of the requisite number of elected members.

Elections to office or to committee, whether at the beginning or at the end of a session, have all been by silent acclamation, although any member could insist on a secret ballot, as provided by Section 16 of the Rules of Procedure.

Section 17 of the Rules defines voting procedure on noncontroversial matters other than recommendations. Section 17(1) permits the presiding officer to assume that a motion or committee proposal is adopted if there is no objection. If opposition has been expressed—e.g., if the committee proposal contains a reservation—then a standing vote is taken pursuant to Section 17(2) of the Rules, and the results are recorded without indicating how the individual members voted. The presiding officer has the tie-breaking vote on these matters. Any elected member may demand a roll-call vote under the provision of Section 17(3) of the Rules of Procedure.

Where alternative proposals have been offered on any measure, the presiding officer may determine—publicly and in advance—the order in which they shall be voted upon, as authorized by Sections 15(3) and 17(2) of the Rules.

On recommendations to the governments, the vote of each member, including the presiding officer, is recorded as required by Article X(1) of the Statute of the Nordic Council. Section 15(2) of the Rules of Procedure allows the elected members to vote for or against a proposed recommendation, or to abstain. As amended in 1962, Section 15(2) goes on to state that a "recommendation is adopted when more than half of those members present who are entitled to vote in the matter have voted yes." Previously, only a simple majority was required. Before 1962, if at least half the members were present, and if all but one abstained, a recommendation could be passed on the favorable vote of one elected member. In practice, such a recommendation would be ignored by the governments.

This was the fate of Recommendation 24/1954, discussed in the next section, which passed by a vote of twenty-four to eight, with thirteen abstentions. Less than one half of the elected membership—which was fifty-three in 1954—voted for the measure. As Item 64/1955, the recommendation was declared to be terminated the following year, even though the governments had taken no action to effectuate it.

The requirement of individually recorded roll-call votes on recommendations is time consuming. In the absence of dissent, it is also tedious, and has led to considerable absence from the floor. At the 1958 session, the Norwegian Christian People's party delegate, Erling Wikborg, noted in general debate that during "the last two days in Helsinki in February 1957 . . . we had . . . 18 roll-calls in which everyone answered yes. The only thing interesting . . . was determining who was absent." [16]

In 1958, the presiding officer attempted to lessen the burden of repetitious voting by calling for simultaneous votes on clusters of matters. Electric voting was used at the 1959 and 1964 sessions in Stockholm, and at the 1962 session in Helsinki. This system is not available in all of the capitals, however, and, in 1959, the novelty led to a considerable number of voting errors.

At the 1961 session in the Danish House of Parliament, which has no voting machines, a new time-saving system of recording votes on recommendations to the governments was tried by the Presidium, following the suggestion of the Interim Committee on Judiciary, which, in turn, borrowed the idea from the Council of Europe. Recognizing the prevalence of unanimity, this system required any member who wanted to vote against a recommendation or to abstain to notify the speaker to that effect. Otherwise, he would record as voting in favor of the recommendation all those who signed the list of attenders at the given meeting. It followed that an elected member need not actually be present on the floor when the vote was taken in order to be recorded positively. Nor would a quorum have to be present, if no one objected. The Rules of Procedure were not amended to accommodate this innovation, but the speaker invoked Section 26, which permits departures from the Rules by a two-thirds majority.

[16] *1958 Record,* p. 66.

In 1962, the original method of taking roll-call votes on individual recommendations was restored. Unanimity still prevails, however, and the similarity between the Nordic Council and the Council of Europe is striking:

> . . . Voting practices . . . constitute one of the peculiarities of international parliamentary assemblies. . . . First, there is a tendency toward the avoidance of showdown situations and hence an unusually large number of votes is unanimous. . . . Second, even the nonunanimous votes show lop-sided majorities. Third, the degree of absenteeism is extraordinary: opposition or indifference to a resolution is often expressed by abstention and absence.[17]

Article X(2) of the Statute of the Nordic Council provides that in "questions which concern certain of the countries exclusively, only the members from those countries may vote." Section 13(3) of the Rules of Procedure extends the operation of this rule into the standing committees. At the first annual session, the Norwegian and Icelandic members considered themselves to be disfranchised on Recommendation 4/1953, regarding the construction of a link across the Sound between Denmark and Sweden. They abstained in committee and on the floor. However, in subsequent years the Norwegian and Icelandic (and later Finnish) members voted on the memoranda which the governments submitted on the action they had taken on this recommendation. Moreover, since 1953, many elected members have voted on matters which have had even less impact on their countries than the Sound crossing would have on Finland, Iceland, and Norway. The question of compulsory abstention was not even raised on these later matters.

Members from unaffected countries have even voted in the face of explicit reference to their remote status. For example, in the consideration of Recommendation 12/1957, relating to cooperation in Lapland, the spokesman for the Standing Committee on Economic Matters noted the following: ". . . as an extraordinary sign of Nordic community and will to work together, [I can state] that Denmark's and Iceland's representatives have announced that they will vote 'yes' even though these countries are obviously not affected to any degree by this motion." [18] Similarly, by amendment

---

[17] Ernst B. Haas, *Consensus Formation in the Council of Europe* (Berkeley and Los Angeles: University of California Press, 1960), p. 15.

[18] *1957 Record,* p. 163.

on the floor the names of the governments of Denmark and Iceland were stricken from the committee proposal which became Recommendation 24/1957, treating with the adjustment of boundaries between Finland, Norway, and Sweden. The committee spokesman, again from the Committee on Economic Matters, added the following comment: "This correction naturally has nothing to do with the right to vote. The Council members from Denmark and Iceland obviously have the right to vote in this matter as well as in all others." [19]

Modification of the rule of disqualification of nonaffected delegations was facilitated by the fact that the recommendations are only advisory. The governments can give them the weight they seem to deserve. Thus, for example, the Danish and Icelandic votes on the boundaries between the other countries would not be persuasive. Furthermore, as a practical matter, it would be awkward to have to evaluate the potential impact of each recommendation on every country, and the resulting frequent disqualification of the Icelandic elected members might prove to be embarrassing.

Nevertheless, Article X(2) has been retained in modified form, to give the elected members of a given country the right to abstain if they choose to do so. This adds little to Section 15(2) of the Rules of Procedure, which permits unqualified and unexplained abstention. The Finnish delegation used Article X(2) as the basis for abstention on Recommendation 27/1958, concerning the establishment of a European Free Trade Area by the OEEC nations. Keeping Article X(2) abstention as a voluntary alternative permitted the Finns to disassociate themselves from a recommendation which might have jarred Finland's sensitive relations with the U.S.S.R.

As will be seen in the next section, however, abstention is used most often as a mild negative vote under Section 15(2) of the Rules, having no connection with Article X(2) disqualification.

Recommendations to the Governments

The end product of Nordic Council deliberations on a given matter, if positive, is a recommendation to the governments. Article X(1) of the Statute states that the "Council shall discuss questions of common interest to the countries and may adopt recommendations to the governments."

[19] *Ibid.,* p. 189.

In the first 9 years of its existence, the Council made 186 recommendations to the governments (see chart 14A). Seventeen of these merely replaced earlier recommendations (see chart 14B). Eighty-four recommendations were considered by the Council to be terminated (see chart 14C). This does not necessarily mean that the results they pointed toward were attained. Termination sometimes indicates only that the Nordic Council no longer considers itself to be the most suitable organ to supervise further action. On other occasions, recommendations have been declared terminated by the Council after a negative reaction from the governments or simply to reduce the number of outstanding recommendations.

CHART 14.

RECOMMENDATIONS TO THE GOVERNMENTS, 1953–61

Annual session in:

	1953	1954	1955	1956	1957	1958	1959	1960	1961	*Total*
A. New Recommendations	9	30	16	21	27	33	24	12	14	186
B. Superseded as of 1961	4	4	3	3	1	1	0	1	—	17
C. Terminated as of 1961	3	20	11	14	20	11	4	1	—	84
D. Balance (A minus B and C)	2	6	2	4	6	21	20	10	14	85

At the end of the 1961 session, there were eighty-five recommendations on which the governments were still expected to report (see chart 14D). The Council passed thirty-three recommendations at the 1962 session, twenty-nine at the 1963 session, thirty at the 1964 session, thirty-eight at the 1965 session, and thirty-one at the 1966 session.

Unanimity is predominant in the adoption of recommendations. Out of the 186 already mentioned, only 25 were opposed by negative votes or weakened by abstentions (see chart 15A). In ten of these twenty-five cases, the opposition consisted merely of one or two elected members (see chart 15B) whose votes may have been fortuitous or whose abstentions may have been based on uncertainty as to which matter was being voted upon. (The instances of negative votes or abstentions whose accidental quality arose out of the use of voting machines at the 1959 session are not included here.) In thirteen of the remaining fifteen cases, three or more elected members refused to support a recommendation after the usual watering-down process had taken place. In only two cases during this period did a *positive* report emerge from committee proposing a recommendation which was still controversial.

Because of their exceptional nature, these two cases highlight the kind of compromise which usually takes place in committee. Eighteen members voted against Recommendation 16/1956, and one member abstained. This measure advocated compulsory conviction for drunken driving on the basis of a uniform alcohol-blood-content standard. Issues of this kind are usually disposed of

CHART 15.

NEGATIVE VOTES AND ABSTENTIONS ON RECOMMENDATIONS, 1953–61

A. Number of recommendations on which dissent occurred at annual session in:

	1953	1954	1955	1956	1957	1958	1959	1960	1961	*Total*
Abstention only	2	3	2	4	0	1	2	1	0	15
Abstention and negative vote	0	2	0	1	0	2	1	1	1	8
Negative vote only	0	1	0	0	0	0	1	0	0	2
Total	2	6	2	5	0	3	4	2	1	25

B. Number of participants in each dissent:

	1953	1954	1955	1956	1957	1958	1959	1960	1961	*Total*
One or two	0	2	2	3	0	1	2	0	0	10
Three or more	2	4	0	2	0	2	2	2	1	15
Total	2	6	2	5	0	3	4	2	1	25

in committee by finding a broad basis of general agreement. For example, Recommendation 17/1956, on the same general subject as Recommendation 16/1956, was adopted unanimously. It proposed that the governments "investigate more closely the question of Nordic cooperation in research in the field of [alcoholic beverages]."

In the same vein, Recommendation 6/1958, which proposed the uniform introduction of daylight saving time, met eight negative votes and three abstentions. If the usual process of finding the lowest common denominator had been imposed in committee, unanimous approval might have been secured for a recommendation to the governments to, say, "work together to investigate the possibility of developing a coordinated policy in the matter of time zones."

Because clear-cut positions had already been taken on the issues of presumptive intoxication and daylight saving time, they did not lend themselves well to the customary process of compromise. The negative votes on Recommendation 6/1958 came primarily from Danish, Finnish, and Swedish agrarians, who traditionally oppose daylight saving time. Similarly, on Recommendation 16/1956, the votes followed previously existing party or national policy. The Danes (except for the Radical Liberals, who are in a minority on this issue in Denmark) and the Icelanders voted against the binding presumption of intoxication, while the Finns, Norwegians, and Swedes voted for it.

In the other thirteen cases of numerically significant dissidence, the minority refused to acquiesce in the committee proposal even after the usual weakening process had been followed. In only two of these—Recommendations 18/1959 and 4/1961—did the dissenters, disgruntled authors, express openly their desire for a stronger recommendation. In the remaining eleven cases, related below, the minority wanted a more negative result than that proposed by the committee.

In the votes on five recommendations, members abstained without taking a stand on the substantive issues involved. Two of these—Recommendations 4/1953 and 27/1958—were based on self-disqualification under Article X(2) of the Statute: the delegations felt that the subject matter of the recommendation did not concern their country. The other three—Recommendations 6/1953, 15/1956, and 1/1960—were based on allegations of premature or unauthorized Council action: that it was improper for a standing committee to tack a proposal for a recommendation to the governments onto a report on Scandinavian cooperation; that the Nordic Council should not presume to instruct cabinet members to arrange meetings among themselves; that a recommendation should not be addressed to a single government.

No recurrent patterns emerge to define the above dissenting groups. Except for some partial cross-national party cohesion among the Conservatives in their objections to Recommendations 6/1953 and 15/1956, the basis for dissent has been primarily national. One or more national delegations voted as a minority unit on Recommendations 4/1953, 16/1956, 6/1958, and 27/1958, while subgroups within a single delegation joined in the dissenting votes on Recommendations 16/1956, 1/1960, and 4/1961. These negative votes have shifted among the countries and the parties.

The remaining instances of dissenting votes on proposed recommendations are not so fluid. They stem consistently from the bourgeois parties of Norway and, later, from the Finnish Communists.

The Liberal, Agrarian, Conservative, and Christian People's parties in Norway have been more or less opposed to Nordic integration. Thus, they were mostly against the establishment of the Nordic Council and have continued to criticize the Council and to argue for its contraction. The Norwegian opposition was also negatively disposed toward a Nordic market (as described in Chapter 6), and has fought other potential incursions on Norwegian independence. No matter how cautious Council recommendations have been on these sensitive subjects, these parties have not acquiesced in them, as can be seen in the following cases.

The eight elected members from the bourgeois parties in Norway voted en bloc against Recommendation 24/1954, which encouraged the extension of absentee ballots to Nordic citizens residing in neighboring Nordic lands. The Norwegians argued that this would require a constitutional amendment in Norway. For the same reason in Denmark, the Danish delegation abstained, with three members absent. The Swedish and Icelandic members favored the recommendation, and the final vote was twenty-four to eight, with thirteen abstentions. The following year, as Item 64/1955, this recommendation was terminated. A similar proposal, Item A 32/1957, was defeated in 1957 on the ground that the registration of voters was essentially an internal matter to be determined by each country for itself. Thus, near unanimity was restored.

With two absences, the Norwegian nonleft again voted as a unit to oppose the mutual exchange of civil servants among the northern countries, as proposed in Recommendation 21/1954. A Danish Conservative and a Swedish Liberal joined the six Norwegians, resisting on principle the idea of giving responsibility and decision-making power to a foreigner. However, the opposition favored an alternative recommendation which supported the subsidization of civil servant's exchange as observers. This example, then, fits in the category of failure to crystallize universal compromise in committee. Similarly, the Norwegian bourgeois parties were united in abstaining, without comment, from the vote on Recommendation 26/1954, which proposed the elimination for Nordic citizens of a residence requirement as a condition of doing business.

On Recommendation 22/1954, which asked the governments to further economic cooperation and "to seek to prepare the ground for the establishment of a common Nordic market," the Norwegian opposition's reservation to Economic Matters Committee Proposal 6/1954 asked for postponement until the next session, to permit the Norwegian Parliament to debate the issue before the Council took action. Voting en masse, the same Norwegian parties stood alone in a dilatory effort, but were joined fortuitously by an Icelandic Agrarian in abstaining from the vote on the merits. Bourgeois Norwegian opposition to the proposed common Nordic market continued in subsequent years, although there was no new recommendation proposed on which to express it. The question finally became moot with Danish, Norwegian, and Swedish adherence to the European Free Trade Association before the 1959 session.

Nineteen fifty-four might be called the year of Norwegian bourgeois dissent. In addition to the four instances just recounted, the Norwegian group was also responsible for the two occurrences of numerically insignificant dissidence that year. Two Norwegian Agrarians abstained on Recommendation 27/1954, which proposed to extend sport fishing rights to all Scandinavians living in any Nordic country. One Norwegian Conservative voted against and one Norwegian Liberal abstained from Recommendation 9/1954, which proposed the creation of a Nordic passport union.

This experience in 1954 was not an exception to the unanimity principle, but rather an assertion of it. The Norwegian opposition made clear that it opposed a common Nordic market, and thus vetoed any positive action. The remaining majority, large as it was, did not attempt to override this veto, which the Norwegian Labor government—with a slender majority which has since disappeared—also respected in the home Parliament. No new recommendation on the common Nordic market was included in a committee proposal until 1958, by which time all-European negotiations overshadowed mere Nordic plans. Recommendation 26/1958 was carefully phrased: it asked the governments "to take up negotiations on the forms for Nordic economic cooperation, with a view to presenting the question to the parliaments when the conditions for a decision are present." The Norwegian opposition had no objection to this proposal.

In attenuated form, the negative attitude of the Norwegian right rose to the surface at the 1960 session. Four of its representatives in the Council—two Conservatives, one Liberal, and the Christian People's party delegate—abstained in the vote on Recommendation 6/1960, which suggested to the governments that they "try to see to what degree a rationalization of the foreign service, particularly in new nations, can be attained through Nordic cooperation." Another Norwegian Conservative and one Norwegian Agrarian voted for the measure. The other Agrarian was absent. No one had opposed a similar and equally precatory measure, Recommendation 8/1959, at the previous session.

As indicated in Chapter 3, a cross section of Norwegian elected members opposed the expansion of the interim committee system at the 1964 session. In 1965, there was a smattering of Norwegian opposition to the uniform patent law proposals in Recommendations 36/1965 and 37/1965. The Icelandic delegation refrained from voting, as the proposals extended only to the four larger countries. The two Liberal and the one Christian People's party representatives abstained from voting on Recommendation 37/1965, which advised the governments to investigate the possibility of setting up a joint court to dispose of appeals in patent cases.

Balancing this modest expression of Norwegian diffidence at the 1965 session was the absence of dissent or abstention on three other proposals entailing rudimentary supranationality. Recommendation 28/1965 urged the governments to enter into a treaty establishing a Nordic Cultural Fund with a combined annual subscription of 3,000,000 Danish crowns (about $425,000), to be placed under joint administration. Recommendation 30/1965 suggested that the governments investigate the possibility of setting up a regional body authorized to make binding decisions on technical questions involving air transportation. Recommendation 31/1965 asked the governments to give preliminary consideration to the creation of a joint authority on technical customs questions.

While Norwegian negativism has declined, a new source of occasional dissent has arisen—dissimilar in political philosophy and less influential in the Council. The four members of the Finnish People's Democratic League absented themselves during the vote on Recommendation 26/1958, discussed above. They did not vote against the recommendation, and they did not formally abstain. No inference could be drawn from this ambiguous action if it were not for the fact that the elected members from this party voted against a similar proposal in 1959, Recommendation 12/1959, which generally proposed continued economic cooperation among the Northern nations. The Communists read issues of imperialism into this bland proposal and voted against it.

The Finnish Communists can be expected to vote as a bloc and to dissent whenever they choose to claim that great power issues are at stake. They did so again in 1961 and 1962. In the latter year, with wavering support from their Danish and Icelandic brethren, they voted against those aspects of Recommendation 24/1962—later to become the Helsinki Agreement, discussed in the next chapter—which had to do with economic cooperation.

The 1961 incident was even more pointed. At the ninth annual session, the Finnish People's Democratic League representatives proposed—as Item A 27/1961—that Scandinavia be declared a zone from which atomic weapons were to be excluded. The Economic Matters Committee asserted that this topic was beyond the competence of the Council, which should continue its policy of avoiding issues connected with national security. The Communist member of the committee offered a minority proposal containing a positive recommendation for the creation of a zone. In debate, the non-Communist participants studiously avoided commenting on the merits of the question, while arguing its inappropriateness for Council consideration. In the vote in which the minority proposal was defeated, the four Finnish Communists were again joined by their solitary Danish and Icelandic counterparts—a clear case of cross-national party cohesion. Five other Finns abstained, to avoid even the appearance of violating the restriction against voting on cold war issues which the Finns had made a condition of their entry into the Council.

The confusion and awkwardness which attended the disposition of this matter led to the 1962 amendment to Section 15(2) of the Rules of Procedure requiring a qualified majority for passage of a recommendation, to prevent its adoption by a simple majority based upon scanty participation in the actual vote.

President Kekkonen of Finland proposed in May, 1963, that the Nordic countries agree to prohibit the introduction of nuclear weapons into the area. This gave the Finnish Communists another occasion to bring the matter before the Nordic Council, as Item A

49/1964 at the 1964 session. The result was much the same as in 1961, except that cross-national party cohesion broke down. The Danish Socialist People's party delegate, Aksel Larsen, offered an alternative proposal, which was rejected twenty-six to one. Larsen abstained from the final vote on the Finnish Communist minority proposal. Four non-Communist Finns also abstained, while seven others were absent. The minority proposal was defeated by forty-nine votes to four, the latter being the entire Finnish People's Democratic League delegation in the Nordic Council. The Icelandic Communist representative was absent on the vote, even though he had voted moments before against the Larsen amendment.

In 1965, the Finnish Communists attempted in Item A 57(e)/1965 to get the Nordic Council to go on record as favoring the admission of East German legislators into the Inter-Parliamentary Union. Though he agreed in principle, Aksel Larsen spoke against the measure on the ground that governments—to whom any recommendation would be directed—were the wrong forum. On the final vote, the four Finnish Democratic People's League representatives were the sole supporters of their own proposal. They also abstained from the vote on Recommendation 25/1965, which called for continued economic cooperation by the Nordic nations within EFTA, working toward increased trade among all the European nations.

So much for dissenting votes and abstentions. The remaining 161 recommendations of the first 9 years were passed without such expressions of difference. Three of the annual sessions were almost completely free from dissent: there were no negative votes cast at the 1953, 1955, or 1957 sessions. The 1957 session was even free from abstention. Since then, two serious expressions of minority steadfastness have been par for each annual session. The unanimity principle is certainly well established in the Nordic Council.

As already noted, the leadership of the Council expressed concern over excessive compromise in committee deliberations. In the same memorandum, the Presidium—speaking through the Swedish secretariat—criticized the absence of controversy in Council debate, as follows:

> Relative unanimity may well be a prerequisite for the solution of a problem, but new questions on which opinions differ must also be taken up and ventilated. . . .

If the Council is to become a lively forum for debate, it is necessary that questions of a more controversial nature be placed on the agenda in coming Sessions.[20]

But perhaps the requirement of near unanimity and the public expression of controversy are mutually exclusive. Scandinavians are fond of describing politics as "the art of the possible." Even mild disagreement in the Nordic Council makes positive action impossible and renders further conversation futile.

CLOSING A SESSION

Section 1(4) of the Rules of Procedure provides that "sessions will terminate when the matters included in the agenda . . . have been finally decided upon or deferred to a later session." When all the committee proposals have been acted upon, the Council proceeds by silent acclamation to empower the Presidium to carry out certain interim functions and to set the time and place for the next session. The President of the Council then declares the session to be closed.

About one month after the end of a session, the recommendations, signed by the President and countersigned by the Chief Clerk, are transmitted to the governments, as required by Section 20 of the Rules of Procedure.

Pursuant to Section 19 of the Rules, a transcript of the public meetings of the Council is kept and published, as approved by the Presidium. The deliberations at each session, together with all the other documents—proposals, memoranda, reports, minutes of committee hearings, and recommendations—constitute the annual record of the Nordic Council.

Since the 1954 session, each government has been assigned a certain number of recommendations for which it is primarily responsible. At the 1955 and 1956 sessions, the Presidium worked out a distribution of recommendations which the governments accepted at a later joint meeting between the Presidium and the Foreign Ministers of the member nations. Since 1957, the Presidium and governmental representatives have met together on the last day of each session and agreed upon a roughly equal division of recommendations. Only a handful have been assigned to Iceland. In an appendix to the 1960 report of the Presidium, the

[20] *1958 Record*, p. 1624.

Council secretariat attempted to specify the duties of the coordinating country,[21] but the governments have not acted forcefully to implement Council recommendations.

According to a comprehensive survey made by the Council secretariat, the Council's recommendations fall into four nearly equal categories: those which have been fulfilled, those which have been partially carried out, those which are receiving preliminary investigation, and those on which nothing has been done.[22]

APPORTIONING EXPENSES

Article XIII(1) of the Statute of the Nordic Council declares that "Each country shall defray the expenses of its own participation in the Council." These expenses include travel and per diem allowances and the maintenance of the national secretariat. Because of the greater distance involved and the probable infrequency of meetings in Iceland, it was suggested in Joint Working Committee following the 1953 session that the pertinent travel expenses of the members of the Icelandic delegation's working committee, including the Icelandic member of the Presidium, should be considered a common expense. A motion to this effect was finally rejected by the Presidium at its meeting of November 8, 1957.

Article XIII(2) of the Statute states that the "Council shall decide how common expenses shall be apportioned." In Section 21 of the Rules of Procedure, the Council has decided that the "cost of printing and other common expenses referred to in Article XIII of the Statute shall be apportioned among the countries in proportion to the number of elected members to the Council. . . . In special cases the Presidium can fix a different apportionment." Iceland has five elected members to the Council, while the other countries each have sixteen. In apportioning expenses, deviations from this 16:16:16:16:5 ratio have been rare.

As an exception to the general rule of apportionment of common expenses, Section 21 of the Rules states that "Each country shall, however, defray the special cost of meetings held in that country." Apportionment of the cost of rooms, maintenance, entertainment, and so forth would be complicated and speculative. Most

[21] "Tillägg I: PM rörande koordinerande lands uppgifter," *1960 Record,* pp. 416–17. See also *1955 Record,* p. 167.

[22] Petrén (ed.), *Nordiska rådets verksamhet 1952–1961,* p. 329.

of the facilities are provided free by the national parliaments. Moreover, rotation of the annual sessions, of interim committee hearings, and of meetings of the Presidium already assures an approximate equality of expenditure.

The major printing cost is that of the annual record of each session. The cost of the mimeographed *Nytt från Nordiska rådet* is also met by apportionment under Section 21 of the Rules. The expense of preparing the journal *Nordisk Kontakt,* however, is governed by a different formula, based roughly on the total number of members of Parliament—who receive the journal free—in each country; Sweden pays 35 per cent of the *Nordisk Kontakt* costs, Denmark, Finland, and Norway pay 20 per cent each, and Iceland pays 5 per cent.

Other common costs are incurred in hiring permanent secretaries for the interim committees and in contracting for *ad hoc* studies of particular matters. Since 1956, the Presidium has included a classification of common expenditures in its yearly report, as part of the section on "Financial Conditions." In the 1961 report, the Presidium added a public estimate of the amounts of common expenditures anticipated for the current year. In 1961, 1962, and 1963, the expected needs were $37,500, $41,500, and $76,000, respectively. In 1964, the amount rose to $89,000, falling to $80,000 in 1965.

Of course, the Council has no taxing power. At its meeting of April 18–19, 1956, the Presidium decided that a periodic statement of common expenditures should be acknowledged in writing by the members of the Presidium on the assumption "That the members of the Presidium from the respective working committees can act to accept the charge which falls on the delegation." [23] This system has worked satisfactorily.

The national delegations themselves have no funds, but must request an appropriation from the parent Parliament. Apart from one modest hint from the Presidium that "perhaps later a change in this point might become timely," [24] the Council has not made an issue of its financial dependence on the national parliaments.

For the first seven years of operation, the total amount appropriated by the five parliaments, covering both joint and several expenses, was slightly less than seven hundred thousand dollars.

[23] *1957 Record,* p. 658.
[24] *Ibid.,* p. 384.

The cost of the Nordic Council has increased from year to year, but it is still an institution of modest proportions. Sweden has spent about twice as much each year as Norway, with Denmark and Finland falling in between. Except in Norway, where the expenses for the Council are attributed to the Department of Foreign Affairs, Nordic Council expenditures are included in the parliaments' own account for a given year.

APPRAISAL

Any elected member or government may offer a proposal for consideration by the Nordic Council. Article I of the Statute states that the "Nordic Council is an organ for consultation between the [parliaments and between] the governments. . . , in matters involving joint action by any or all of the countries." Unlike the Nordic Inter-Parliamentary Union, which usually limited itself to a few topics of broad general interest where no immediate legislation was envisaged, the Nordic Council has undertaken to consider a larger number of specific problems which might lend themselves to a common solution. As these latter proliferate, voices are heard urging a return to the more philosophical debates which characterized the predecessor organ. For example, the secretariat has suggested that the Council might take up the problem of juvenile delinquency. This could be done under the aegis of Article X of the Statute, which provides that the "Council shall discuss questions of common interest to the countries. . . ."

While there is no limitation on topics which the Council may consider, fundamental differences in foreign policy among the member nations have led to the selective exclusion of that subject from the Council agenda. Disappointment over the failure to form a Scandinavian Defense Alliance gave rise to the Nordic Council in the first place. With rare exception, proposals touching on extra-Scandinavian political and military policies simply have not been introduced. On the other hand, the Council has regularly entertained questions relating to Scandinavian economic relations with the rest of the world.

The forbidden area seems to be limited to cold war issues. The Finns have given formal expression to the restriction which is otherwise defined only in practice. When the Finnish government introduced a proposition into Parliament in 1955, asking preliminary approval of the government's decision to seek membership in the Nordic Council, it included the following cautionary statement of policy:

> . . . if the Council, contrary to established practice, should take up the consideration of questions of national defense or questions which lead to the taking of positions in the conflict of interests between the Great Powers, then Finland's representatives ought not take part in the consideration of these questions.[25]

The Finnish People's Democratic League clearly violated the spirit of this injunction in offering its proposal in 1961 and subsequent years for the creation of a nonnuclear Nordic zone. Nevertheless, the Finnish restriction recognizes the universal subject matter competence of the Council and the voluntary nature of limitations on it.

The complete permissiveness of the rules governing the introduction of matters has sometimes resulted in an agenda burdened with numerous but relatively unimportant items. The single criticism most frequently leveled at the Nordic Council, whether by its friends or its opponents, has been that it is a "paper-mill," too encumbered by a mass of trivial documents to give attention to really important matters. The response to this complaint has not been to restrict formally the right of members to introduce matters, or to lessen the duty of the governments to submit reports, but has rather been an attempt to handle routine matters more expeditiously. At the same time, the avoidance of controversy which characterizes the Council tends to make all matters routine. Thus, the evolution of Council procedure has been that of successive accommodation to the unanimity principle.

This accommodation is reflected more strikingly in the disappearance of debate on first reading and in the 1961 reduction to a mere formality of votes on recommendations to the governments. Otherwise, the changes have been modest in scope.

At the 1964 session, the Presidium (except for the Icelandic member) authored Item A 24/1964, which proposed to eliminate the nine-man interim committees by putting the standing committees on a year-round basis and authorizing them to decide when and whether to return matters to the floor of Council-in-session.

The Interim Committee on Judiciary agreed that such a change would undercut criticism by reducing drastically the number of

[25] *Reg. prp.* (Regeringsproposition), 82/1955, p. 1.

items on each sessional agenda. At the same time, the committee was apprehensive that de-emphasis of standing committee hearings at the annual sessions might disturb the relations with ministers and civil servants which the Council had built up over the years.

Consequently, the interim committee recommended that the Presidium's proposal be tested provisionally through suspension of the Rules under Section 26. If the new system should prove to be effective and not disruptive of Council-government rapport, then the Statute and Rules could be amended accordingly. With the encouragement of ministerial representatives, the Council adopted the interim committee recommendation, and the experiment is now under way.

The results at the 1965 session were inconclusive. The sessional agenda was crowded, and there was some complaint that the Standing Committee on Communications had neglected the governments in its interim deliberations on the Sound crossing proposals which culminated in Recommendations 34/1965 and 35/1965.

By 1966, year-round operation of the standing committees was generally accepted. It was approved, for example, by a special working committee, composed of ten elected members and the secretariat, which the Presidium set up following the 1966 session to study Council procedures. Even though successful, the change in committee structure will not be revolutionary. In the 1961 report of the Presidium, the secretariat noted that:

> The question of the Nordic Council's position, and so on, is not in the first instance to be seen as a technical problem (concerning the procedures of the Council and that sort of thing). The future place which the Nordic Council is to take in the lives of the Nordic states turns on the position these states take towards Nordic cooperation. As long as this question is not posed and answered, continued discussion of minute organizational questions hangs in the air.[26]

This circumlocution means that the governments must become Nordic activists if the Council is ever to assume a meaningful role in Scandinavian politics. So far, all efforts to engage the governments in the work of the Council have failed, as will be seen in the succeeding paragraphs.

The governments have not responded effectively to repeated

[26] *1961 Record,* p. 1196.

requests that they introduce matters into the Council. Governmental proposals have been relatively few, and have usually pertained to topics of secondary importance. Until 1959, governmental proposals asked the Council only for an expression of views. As a gesture of compliance with the request of the Presidium, the governments have subsequently made requests for recommendations in a few of their proposals, but even these are usually phrased in quite general terms.

The governments have not joined seriously in debate. Almost none of the vital exchange between front and back bench which typifies the national parliaments has occurred in the sessions of the Nordic Council.

The governments have been conscientious in submitting memoranda on action taken on Council recommendations and reports on Scandinavian cooperation. Many of the former are quite uninformative, however, and the governments have not responded markedly to the Presidium's plea that they formulate memoranda "so that the Council will have clear information as to the Governments' standpoint and motivation." [27] Nils Andrén points out that the duty to submit memoranda "is in itself a certain pressure on the Governments to ensure that they really have something to report to the Council. It must, however, be admitted," he adds, "that this pressure many times has been too inefficient to produce rapid and constructive results." [28]

As far as the reports on Scandinavian cooperation are concerned, the governments have merely acted as conduits through which the administrative organs of Nordic cooperation have reported, and have avoided the expression of official governmental views.

Finally, the governments have been passive in their response to repeated requests from the Presidium that they help plan the work of the Council, sessional and interimistic.

If the Nordic Council should ever assume an authoritative role in the decision-making process in matters of Scandinavian intergovernmental cooperation, as urged in the 1966 program of the Union of Norden Societies, radical changes in Council procedure would result.

[27] *1962 Record*, p. 1403.
[28] Nils Andrén, *Government and Politics in the Nordic Countries* (Stockholm: Almqvist and Wiksell, 1964), p. 216.

First of all, simultaneous translation of Council debates in plenary session and in committee would be necessary. The usefulness of this service to Finnish-speaking and Icelandic-speaking members is obvious. Those who speak Danish, Norwegian, and Swedish would also benefit. While these three languages are mutually comprehensible after acclimatization, the level of comprehension does not usually attain that subtle mastery of language which is required for lawmaking. Written language is less deceptive, and the annual record might well keep its present untranslated trilingual form. An Icelandic synopsis on the order of the already-existing Finnish summary of the record might be advisable.

Eventually, elected members of the Council might not be members of Parliament. One week a year is inadequate for the meaningful exercise of a truly legislative function. As long as the Council is composed of members of Parliament, however, it will be difficult to find more time than this. Moreover, the Council has already experienced difficulty in finding a season which is convenient for the representatives of all five parliaments. If the members of the Council were not members of Parliament, both of these problems would be solved. Conceivably, nongovernmental members of the Council might even be chosen directly by the electorates, instead of by the legislatures. At present, it is the members of Parliament who— together with the ministerial representatives—lend prestige to the Nordic Council. If the decisions of the Council were binding on the member states, the Council would no longer be dependent on the reputations which its members have gained elsewhere.

A supranational Nordic Council would profit from a central secretariat, preferably not in one of the capitals. Iceland, the Luxemburg of Scandinavia, is too remote, and the choice of any other capital might give rise to jealousy. The five national secretariats should by all means be retained. The creation of a Nordic capital would permit the establishment of a sorely needed central archive of Nordic Council documents and depository of national documents relating to matters of Scandinavian cooperation. The central secretariat could supervise the editorial functions of the Council. It might encourage the timely introduction of matters into the Council, and their prompt distribution to the members. It would also arrange, in cooperation with the national bureaus, for Nordic Council meetings of all kinds, and would provide a home base for the Presidium and the interim committees—although there is no reason why the meetings themselves should not continue to be held throughout Scandinavia. In addition to the positive tasks it would assume, the creation of an independent headquarters would end the domination of the Swedish and Danish secretariats, which might otherwise become a source of resentment. As a tinder to kindle Norwegian enthusiasm, perhaps the headquarters should be located in that country.

If the elected members to the Council were not members of Parliament, they would have to be salaried. Travel expenses would also have to be assumed by the Council, together with the responsibility for the maintenance of the all-Nordic secretariat. Thus, supranationality would require financial independence in some degree. This could be accomplished by treaty whereby the member states bind themselves to make fixed contributions or to provide the Council with a limited tax base like that given to the European Coal and Steel Community. The Council would then have to add to its agenda the consideration of its own budget.

With the emergence of the Nordic Council as a new center of decision-making power in Scandinavia, the governments would have to assert themselves in the introduction of matters and in debate. The Council would lose its purely interparliamentary aspect. Swedish hegemony in drafting bills would probably decrease. Controversy would appear in the Council, both in committee and on the floor. Measures which today emerge as precatory or dilatory would more often be defeated, while those positive proposals which now find unanimous or near-unanimous support would become law. The Presidium and the Secretaries-General would be the servants of the Council instead of its master—but they would be serving a legislature, rather than leading a debating society. Finally, patterns of cross-national party cohesion or other coalitions of some permanence would emerge to give character to the Council.

The conjecture in the preceding paragraphs is presented neither as prescription nor prediction. It is not assumed here that Scandinavia would be a better or worse place with a supranational Nordic Council. The description of the form which an authoritative Council might take serves merely to underline the present nonauthoritative status of the Council, to which the Council's procedures are adapted. Let it be emphasized that this is the kind of Council which the governments agreed to create in 1952. They have never purported to change its basic nature. Until they do, legislative procedure in the Nordic Council will continue to express the unanimity principle which is characteristic of consultative assemblies when discussing anything except their own future.

Chapter Five

THE NORDIC COUNCIL
AND THE GOVERNMENTS

The Nordic Council has many competitors, public and private, in the domain of inter-Scandinavian cooperation. Before World War II, techniques of intergovernmental collaboration were largely informal.[1] Since the end of that war, a number of official bodies for regional cooperation have come into being. These organs vary greatly in size, composition, and duration. Just as on the legislative side, those which stem from the executive branch are a continuation and expansion of prewar endeavors.

There has been a continuing increase in the frequency of joint meetings of corresponding cabinet members. Partly to coordinate United Nations policy, the Foreign Ministers meet twice a year. The Ministers of Justice get together annually, the Ministers of Social Welfare and the Ministers of Education gather every other year, and the Ministers of Fisheries convene every third year. The holders of some other portfolios meet irregularly, in addition to their confrontations at the annual sessions of the Nordic Council and at the all-Nordic conferences of fraternal political parties, particularly those of the Social Democratic parties. The Prime Ministers also meet with the Presidium of the Nordic Council in advance of each annual session.

Except for those of the Foreign Ministers, decisions reached by

[1] They are surveyed by Eric C. Bellquist, "Inter-Scandinavian Cooperation," *The Annals of the American Academy of Political and Social Science,* CLXVIII (July, 1933), 183–94.

the ministers at their joint meetings are not effectively implemented. The Nordic Council has not succeeded in remedying this defect. At the Harpsund conference in October, 1960, the Presidium suggested to the Prime Ministers that one year should be the minimal interval for meetings of corresponding ministers. It was felt that frequent meetings would stimulate administrative attention to ministerial directives. While delicately phrased, the reaction of the Danish Prime Minister, Viggo Kampmann, was negative. He felt that ministerial conference "ought to be extended gradually, as the need reveals itself." [2] Council Recommendation 15/1956 met a similar fate. It advised the governments to have the Ministers of Health meet "as needed." The ministers met once, two years later, after which the Council declared the recommendation to be terminated.

Greater formality has been imposed on ministerial meetings connected with economic cooperation. Pursuant to Nordic Council Recommendation 22/1954, the governments of Denmark, Norway, and Sweden each named a cabinet member—in Denmark, the Minister of Labor and Economic Planning; in Norway and Sweden, the Ministers of Commerce—to assume "responsibility for the preparation of matters concerning Nordic economic cooperation." These three were called the Ministers of Economic Cooperation. In August, 1956, the government of Finland appointed the Finance Minister to this body.

In Recommendation 12/1959, following the breakdown of negotiations for a common Nordic market, the Council asked the governments "to create . . . adequate machinery [for the] further development of economic cooperation." The governments of all five countries proceeded to replace the 1954 Ministers of Economic Cooperation with a new Nordic Ministerial Committee for Economic Cooperation, consisting of the same cabinet posts. For all practical purposes, these two ministerial committees can be considered as one. The ministers meet on their own initiative, as often as four or five times a year.

The Nordic Council is represented at many of the joint meetings of Scandinavian cabinet members, including those of the Ministers of Education, Social Welfare, Health, and Justice. In 1953 and

[2] *Nordisk Råd: 9. session, 1961* ("The Nordic Council: Ninth Session, 1961," hereinafter cited as *1961 Record;* the other annual records will be similarly cited), p. 1187.

1954, the Presidium itself met with the Ministers of Education. Since then, the Council has turned this function over to the ordinary elected members and to the Secretaries-General. Representatives of the Council's Committee on Judiciary meet regularly with the Ministers of Justice after the latter's joint meetings are terminated. The other ministers permit the Council's representatives to attend the primary meetings directly.

Ministers also attend some interim meetings of the Council's committees. In December, 1960, the members of the Nordic Ministerial Committee for Economic Cooperation attended the sessions of the Interim Committees on Judiciary and Economic Matters. It is a recent custom for the latter committee to receive an oral report on common market negotiations from a suitable cabinet member in the country where the committee is meeting.

After the standing committees assumed interim functions in 1964, the appropriate cabinet members attended the dispositive committees meetings which preceded the 1965 session.

Increased contacts among Scandinavian civil servants have kept pace with those of their political chiefs. While much Nordic administrative coordination takes place on an *ad hoc* basis, some administrators have established continuous contact with their opposite numbers; these tend to acquire reciprocal linguistic and bureaucratic acclimatization. According to the Danish Nordic Council secretariat, "Agency heads meet quite frequently. This is true for the top leaders of the postal service, the telegraph service, the state railways, the departments of health, the customs agencies and the commerce sections of the Foreign Ministries." [3]

Barriers to communication have been broken down. Official letters and printed materials sent by civil servants in one Scandinavian country to those in another are not subject to customs inspection. Moreover, government officials in the Nordic countries may telephone, write, or visit their neighboring opposite numbers without using their respective Foreign Offices:

> The local authorities in the several countries [may correspond directly] in matters of social welfare benefits, tax collection, collection of census data, etc. . . . Agencies of the central government may also as a rule [correspond] directly, [unless] relations with other

[3] Danish Nordic Council Secretariat, "Nogle resultater af Nordisk samarbejde gennem 15 år, 1945–60" (mimeographed release No. 197, August 23, 1960), p. 5.

countries outside Scandinavia or considerations of internal coordination militate against it. . . .[4]

Informal contacts among governmental officials have also multiplied in the postwar period. Denmark, Norway, and Sweden have established a modest program for the temporary exchange of civil servants, who work for a year or less in a corresponding neighboring agency.

Nearly one hundred governmental officials attend the annual sessions of the Nordic Council as advisers to the Council or to the governments. When serving as host country, Denmark, Finland, or Sweden supply from one third to one half of the total. Otherwise, Sweden usually sends more advisers than Denmark or Finland, and they in turn each send more than Norway. Iceland accounts for only one or two. According to the Secretary-General of the Norwegian Nordic Council delegation:

> The purpose [of the presence of the experts at the Nordic Council's Sessions is to] express their views on the possibilities of carrying out a proposed Recommendation. One has also felt it to be important to get the experts engaged in the Council's work, because it is they who in the first instance from the Governments' side will process the Recommendations which are adopted at the Session. . . . The number of experts in the meantime has perhaps become too large. At the last Session [1963], one of the countries had twice as many experts as parliamentarians, while Norway, for example, has tried to limit herself to one expert for each Council Committee. A certain harmonization among the countries in the number of experts could perhaps be in order.[5]

In a more highly structured form, civil servants come together as departmental representatives on the permanent organs of cooperation—the Nordic Cultural Commission, the Nordic Social Welfare Committee, and the Nordic Committee for Economic Cooperation. These commissions have no direct executive authority, but serve as investigatory bodies whose duties are discharged when they report to the governments.

The Nordic Cultural Commission was first proposed at the Nordic Inter-Parliamentary Union's meeting of delegates in August, 1946. The initial meeting of the commission was held in June,

[4] *1956 Record,* p. 119.
[5] Einar Løchen, "Arbeidsformene i Nordisk Råd og Europarådet," *Nordisk Kontakt,* No. 8 (1963), p. 441.

1947. After 1954, when it was first reorganized, the commission consisted of six members from each of the five countries.[6] Two members from each country served on each of three ten-man sections. Section one treated with higher education and scientific matters; section two was responsible for matters relating to the public schools; section three covered art and popular education and assumed residual jurisdiction over miscellany. Two members of each national group were members of Parliament and another represented the national department of education. The remaining members were distinguished private citizens.

The sections usually met twice a year, once in connection with the plenary meeting of the commission. Each national group elected a chairman, and the chairmen constituted a Presidium. The presidency of the commission rotated every other year among the chairmen of the groups, and the secretary to the group supplying the president acted as commission secretary-general. The three sections were chaired by commission members from each of the other three countries, excluding Iceland. Section chairmen were not members of the Presidium, even though the sections were the actual working bodies of the commission. The commission had no independent investigatory staff other than the nine part-time secretaries of sections and groups. A civil servant in the Ministry or Department of Education was assigned responsibility for liaison.

According to Håkan Branders, formerly secretary to the Finnish group in the commission, the plenary meetings did not assume a general supervisory function, but merely ratified the reports of the sections. Branders also complained of the lack of contact between the commission and the domestic administrative agencies—the same barrier which frustrates the Nordic Council. Moreover, he asserted, the commission remained isolated from the Nordic Council and from other Nordic organs by the requirement that it communicate through the governments. The Nordic Cultural Commission was reorganized in 1962.[7] Håkan Branders has since become

[6] See Nils Andrén, "The Nordic Cultural Commission, 1947–1957," *The Norseman*, XV, No. 6 (November-December, 1957), 375–82; and Gunnar Christie Wasberg, "The Nordic Cultural Commission," *The American-Scandinavian Review*, XLIX, No. 2 (June, 1961), 169–73.

[7] Håkan Branders, "Kultursamarbetet i blickpunkten," *Nordisk Kontakt*, No. 8 (1962), pp. 431–34. The author urged that the commission, the Nordic Council, and the Ministers of Education act to remedy the cited defects, just as they had previously joined to reform the commission in 1954.

secretary to the Nordic Council Committee on Cultural Affairs. *The Nordic Social Welfare Committee,* which first met in 1951, consists of two civil servants from the Departments of Social Welfare of Denmark, Finland, Norway, and Sweden, and one from Iceland. Kaare Salvesen describes the committee as follows:

> [It] is composed of two or three officials from each country, usually permanent heads of departments dealing with social security, labour or general welfare, including the family. The [Committee] may have two or three sessions in the year. The great majority of proposals for new forms of co-operation that are presented from various quarters pass through this body, which also prepares the agenda for the Meetings of the Ministers of Social Affairs.[8]

There have been three successive committees of experts in the field of economic cooperation. *The Joint Nordic Committee for Economic Cooperation* was set up by the governments of Denmark, Iceland, Norway, and Sweden in February, 1948, consisting of from one to three members from each country, usually higher civil servants.

The Joint Committee was superseded by the *Nordic Economic Cooperation Committee* in October, 1954, at the same time that the governments of Denmark, Norway, and Sweden appointed Ministers of Economic Cooperation. The new committee consisted of three members and a secretary from each of the three countries, all of whom were civil servants in the Foreign Office, Department of Commerce, Department of Finance, or related agency of their home country. They secured the assistance of a score of other civil servants and private consultants on subcommittees. In August, 1956, Finland added three members to the committee.

The committee was extremely active during the period of European free trade area negotiations in 1957 and 1958. It held seventeen meetings during this period, while the secretariat held thirty. In addition, twenty-four special committees with their own staff gathered for a total of sixty-five meetings.[9]

The staff for all these meetings included approximately twenty

[8] Kaare Salvesen, "Co-operation in Social Affairs Between the Northern Countries of Europe," *International Labour Review,* LXXIII, No. 4 (April, 1956), 354. See also *Nordic Co-operation in the Social and Labour Field* (Denmark: Rosenborg, 1965).

[9] See *1958 Record,* p. 1255.

Norwegian civil servants, more than forty Danish and more than forty Swedish civil servants and consultants, and about sixty-five Finnish governmental officials and experts. The end result of this prodigious activity was a series of reports totaling over eighteen hundred pages, reprinted as a supplementary volume to the official record of the 1958 session. The comprehensive information in these studies has been used in evaluating all of the proposals for economic cooperation which the Scandinavians have considered.

The Nordic Economic Cooperation Committee underwent a formal transformation in late 1959 or early 1960 as a consequence of the substitution of the new Ministerial Committee for Economic Cooperation in place of the Ministers of Economic Cooperation. At the same time, some changes in membership were effected in the Economic Cooperation Committee, and three Icelanders were added to it.

The Nordic Uniform Law Committee was founded in 1946 with two members and a secretary each from Denmark, Finland, Iceland, Norway, and Sweden. The members were either high officials in the Ministries of Justice, Supreme Court judges, or professors of law. The committee met annually until its quiet dissolution in 1960 or 1961. At present, one civil servant in each national Department or Ministry of Justice is responsible for liaison in matters of uniform law.[10]

For nearly a century, the legal profession itself has been primarily responsible for parallel legislation. The greatest progress has been made in the fields of commercial law, family law, and—most recently—criminal law. Frederik Vinding Kruse criticized the slow pace of legal cooperation, estimating that "we shall not acquire a Northern Civil Code until after the year 2000." [11] Kruse attributed the slowness to the fact that each topic was given to a ten- to fifteen-member special committee which met at long intervals over a period of many years.

In addition to the permanent organs of cooperation, corresponding to four of the five standing committees of the Nordic Council

[10] See "Nordic Co-operation in the Legal Field," an address given by Hans Hækkerup, Danish Minister of Justice, to the Consultative Assembly of the Council of Europe, September 20, 1963, mimeographed by the Danish Nordic Council secretariat as release No. 110 (Oct. 9, 1963).

[11] Frederik Vinding Kruse, *A Nordic Draft Code* (Copenhagen: Munksgaard, 1963), p. xv.

(Cultural Affairs, Social Policy, Economic Matters, and Judiciary), there have been a number of special committees. As examples, the Danish Nordic Council secretariat lists the following:

> . . . the Nordic Committee on the Common Labor Market, the Nordic Committee on Research in Communications, the Nordic Consultative Committee on Questions of Atomic Energy, the Nordic Committee on Aliens, the Nordic Committee on Social Statistics, the Nordic Committee for Uniform Statistics on Wages, and the Nordic Committee on Comparison in Costs of Living.[12]

It was never intended that the Nordic Council would replace the administrative organs of cooperation. Nonetheless, Hans Hedtoft had expected that the Council would coordinate the activities of these bodies:

> When a commission of experts has completed the preparation of a particular matter . . . [it] ought to be sent to the Nordic Council before being transmitted to the several Governments, so that [the Council would] become a kind of coordinating organ, which would intercept whatever came from the . . . experts, rework it and examine the possibilities of [success] in the several parliaments.[13]

It has not done so. Hedtoft's efforts to have the permanent organs of cooperation report directly to the Nordic Council were of no avail; they report to the Council through the governments, and receive their instructions from the governments.

Perhaps the Nordic Council has had difficulty in making a place for itself in Nordic collaboration precisely because there was such a complete network for cooperation existing before its creation. Rather than dissipate energy in jurisdictional disputes, the Presidium and secretariats of the Nordic Council have chosen to work directly on the governments for the effectuation of Council policy. The techniques have been two-fold: infiltration and lobbying. In short, the Nordic Council has operated as a pressure group. In general debate at the twelfth annual session, Swedish Prime Minister Tage Erlander stated: "I believe that every Cabinet Member ought to be able to provide examples of how the Nordic Council in reality has served as an effective *pressure group,* sometimes irritat-

---

[12] "Nogle resultater af Nordisk samarbejde gennem 15 år, 1945–60," p. 5.
[13] In debate on first reading of the bill for adoption by Denmark of the Statute of the Nordic Council, *Folk. forh.* (May 15, 1952), col. 4409.

ing and troublesome—that I will not deny—but often extraordinarily useful." [14] The present author argues that the successful imposition of pressure by the Council is relatively rare.

Lobbying has been both direct and indirect. The success of the former depends upon the reliability and persuasiveness of the buttonholer. Nordic Council representatives—primarily the Secretaries-General—are eminently trustworthy and have the requisite information at their disposal. They have not, however, been able to convince decision-makers of the importance of Nordic issues, which, except for the proposed common market, have always been overshadowed by domestic problems. The merits of Nordic Council recommendations are seldom debated in the national legislatures.

To break this impasse, the Danish Secretary-General, aided by the Norden Societies (discussed in the concluding chapter), has attempted to reach the politicians indirectly by molding public opinion. Feedback from press release to public to politican has not been effective. Statements to the contrary must be viewed as efforts to create the atmosphere which they ostensibly claim to describe.

Such is the construction which should be given to Hans Hedtoft's remarks at the 1951 meeting of delegates of the Nordic Inter-Parliamentary Union:

> It is my definite impression that, far from wondering why we took the initiative for negotiations [for the creation of a Nordic Council], there is a growing surprise and a growing impatience among our peoples over the fact that more does not happen and that greater results are not obtained in those areas of Nordic cooperation where the Governments and parliaments have responsibility.[15]

Creation of the Nordic Council itself can be viewed in part as an attempt to stimulate public opinion. If it had not been for Hedtoft's desire to produce a psychological counterweight to the disillusionment which followed the abandonment of the Scandinavian Defense Alliance, his purposes could have been met by openly revamping the Nordic Inter-Parliamentary Union.

[14] *1964 Record*, p. 56. (Italics added; the italicized words were spoken in English.)
[15] *Redogörelse för 28 nordiska interparlamentariska delegerademötet år 1951*, p. 25.

A similar use of the phoenix effect is seen in the establishment of new or reshuffled organs after the 1959 demise of common Nordic market plans: the Nordic Ministerial Committee for Economic Cooperation, the revised Nordic Economic Cooperation Committee, and the Nordic Council Interim Committee on Economic Matters. Likewise, in 1962, unilateral Danish application for membership in the European Economic Community led to the Helsinki Agreement on Nordic Cooperation, discussed below. The proliferation of official programs of cooperation has served as a substitute for integration: "[The Nordic Council's] techniques of operation suggest that there may be an inverse ratio between the desire for greater unity, on the one hand, and the elaboration of institutions, on the other." [16]

The citizens of the five countries continue to look to their separate national governments for the solutions to problems, and the Nordic Council has not been able to establish its own constituency. While Gallup polls in Denmark in 1956 showed that 87 per cent of those asked wanted more cooperation in cultural and economic areas, and 72 per cent wanted more in the political arena, yet only slightly more than half had heard of the proposed common Nordic market.[17] By 1957, 65 per cent of the Danes had heard of the Nordic market plans, and two thirds of these felt that they were to Denmark's economic advantage.[18] In Finland, a 1954 Gallup poll indicated that four in ten wanted to retain Scandinavian cooperation, while an additional four in ten wanted to expand it.[19] In 1960, however, 33 per cent of those Finns asked knew about the European Free Trade Association, while only 16 per cent could name the erstwhile proposed common Nordic market.[20] Numerous Norwegian Gallup polls displayed a similar though less emphatic positive response to Nordic cooperation, but also showed that Norwegians were skeptical of specific plans for economic integration, whether European or Scandinavian in scope. When asked late in 1957 if they favored economic cooperation, half had no opinion; of the other half, 20 per cent wanted Nordic economic

---

[16] Ruth C. Lawson, *International Regional Organizations: Constitutional Foundations* (New York: Praeger, 1962), p. 199.

[17] Dansk Gallup Institut, Ugens Gallup No. 37/1956.

[18] *Ibid.*, No. 28/1957.

[19] Suomen Gallup Osakeyhtiö article dated Nov. 18, 1954.

[20] *Ibid.*, article dated Feb. 4, 1960.

cooperation, 18 per cent urged European economic cooperation, while 12 per cent opposed both forms of economic cooperation.[21]

While the great mass of informed Scandinavians approves of cooperation and even wants it to increase, the number of voters who know about and favor specific proposals for new Nordic organs of supranational character usually falls well short of half. Nor would a bare majority be sufficient to carry out such a radical change.

As a force external to government, then, the Nordic Council has been able to rally little effective support. Consequently, the leadership has turned its efforts toward integrating the Council into the administrative apparatus, toward making the Council an intergovernmental organ as well as an interparliamentary one.

The policy, established in 1954, of assigning Council recommendations to a particular government has been ineffective. The responsible government has not, for the most part, either stimulated action or established liaison. The failure of the governments to consult the Council in 1959 when they abandoned the proposed common Nordic market for individual entry into the European Free Trade Association provided a political basis for an attempt to force the governments to overcome administrative inertia. Venting their displeasure at the 1959 session, it seemed as if the opposition parties in Denmark (led by the Conservative Ole Bjørn Kraft) and Sweden (led by the Liberal Bertil Ohlin, President of the Council) might make a domestic issue of the governments' cavalier treatment of the Nordic aspects of common market negotiations.[22]

The Presidium insisted that the Prime Ministers meet with them to iron out the future status of the Council, particularly its relationship with the governments. At the customary joint meeting of Presidium and ministerial representatives which accompanied the 1960 session, Prime Minister Tage Erlander of Sweden extended

---

[21] Gallup poll dated December 28, 1957. Additional polls on attitudes toward Nordic cooperation, with equally tentative conclusions, may be found in Knut Dahl Jacobsen, Stein Rokkan, and Normann Vetti, *Kontakt og Samarbeid mellom de Nordiske Folk* (Oslo: mimeographed by Institutt for Samfunnsforskning, 1956), pp. 65–69, 78–80.

[22] Peter H. Merkl notes a similar use of European assemblies as a forum in which the spokesmen "of parties which are in opposition at home . . . air general criticisms of the foreign policies of their governments," in his "European Assembly Parties and National Delegations," *Journal of Conflict Resolution,* VIII, No. 1 (March, 1964), 54.

an invitation for a meeting at Harpsund on October 6–7, 1960. Anticipating this meeting, the Council secretariats prepared a memorandum which included proposals for institutional reforms. Among these were the establishment of Ministries of Nordic Affairs in the several cabinets, possibly staffed by the Nordic Council national secretariats, which would then become administrative as well as parliamentary adjuncts. It was also proposed that permanent staff be provided to service the joint meetings of corresponding ministers, and that Council representation at these meetings be regularized.

The Harpsund conference was attended by the Prime Ministers (except that Iceland was represented by Emil Jónsson, Minister of Social Welfare and Fisheries) and the five Presidium members, accompanied by the Secretaries-General. The vice-chairman of the Norwegian delegation, Chr. H. Holm, was present as an observer for the Norwegian bourgeois parties.

The resulting protocol revealed no promise of reform save that similar meetings would be held annually to plan upcoming sessions. This was not really an innovation, but represented a resumption of the meetings between the Presidium and the Foreign Ministers which had been held yearly until 1956, to coordinate governmental consideration of Council recommendations. These meetings, which usually took place several months after an annual session, were replaced in 1957 by conferences at the end of the annual sessions, at which all of the ministerial representatives were welcome. Again, the proliferation of institutions was used as a consolation for the refusal to alter inter-Scandinavian relations. The Prime Ministers now meet with the Presidium a few months before each annual session.

In the Harpsund protocol, the Prime Ministers agreed to cooperate in making the work of the Council more effective. But the requests of the Council had been for specific reforms, while the responses of the governments were general or dilatory. In spite of this blandness, the Norwegian Conservative, Holm, disassociated himself from the protocol. Later, in January, 1961, the Danish Prime Minister, Viggo Kampmann, circulated a memorandum to his cabinet colleagues to tell them that they need not meet with their neighboring counterparts any more often than they felt was necessary, and that they could decide for themselves the extent to which they wanted the presence of Council representatives.

In the meantime, help came from another quarter. In September, 1960, one week before the Harpsund conference, the Finnish Prime Minister, V. J. Sukselainen, set up a Ministerial Committee for Nordic Council Affairs, consisting of the holders of five important portfolios, with the Prime Minister as chairman. He also appointed prominent civil servants to be responsible for Nordic Council matters in each of eighteen ministries and departments. In addition, a Coordinating Committee was formed, composed of the Finnish Nordic Council Secretary-General, the Secretary to the Ministerial Committee (who was at the same time responsible for Nordic liaison in the Ministry of Justice), and the Nordic affairs officer from the Ministry of Finance.

After the Harpsund meeting, the Norwegians and Swedes responded to the Finnish innovation by appointing contact men in their own administrative organs. The Norwegians also designated an official in the Prime Minister's office to coordinate Nordic Council matters. The Danes did not follow suit, but indicated that inquiries on Nordic matters would continue to go through the office of the Prime Minister, rather than directly to the agencies concerned. As Prime Minister in 1953, Hans Hedtoft put Nordic Council affairs in his own portfolio because he did not consider them to be "foreign" affairs and because he wanted to expedite them. In 1960, the Danish government used the same arrangement to insulate itself from the rest of Scandinavia, because it feared that closer ties might prejudice the Danish application for membership in the European Economic Community. (The Danish Prime Minister relinquished his hold on Nordic matters in the fall of 1964. They were taken over by the Minister of Economic Planning, who was already responsible for Scandinavian economic cooperation by virtue of his membership on the Nordic Ministerial Committee.)

Establishing contact between opposite numbers in the central administrations was characterized by the Nordic Council secretariat as the most important thing it hoped to accomplish at Harpsund.[23] In the absence of structural coordination, the success of a given proposal for Scandinavian cooperation depends on the willingness and ability of individual political leaders to carry the matter through the national bureaucracies. This has not yet been changed by the Finnish, Norwegian, and Swedish efforts to stimulate the administrative agencies toward regular and earnest consid-

[23] *1961 Record,* p. 1200.

eration of the Nordic aspects of policy formulation and effectuation. The Nordic Council leadership commenced another offensive in August, 1961, when the Presidium instructed the secretariats to prepare a draft treaty on Nordic cooperation for Council consideration at the upcoming tenth annual session early in 1962. The secretariats' draft was transmitted to the governments, whose experts reworked it, and, in so doing, deleted all the binding provisions. The revised version was offered as a governmental proposal, and was adopted by the Council as Recommendation 24/1962. Cabinet members from each of the five countries initialed the treaty on the spot, and it was dubbed the Helsinki Agreement.[24]

Offering the consolation that "he who strives for much often loses all" ("den som fikar efter mycket ofta mister hela stycket"), the Finnish President of the Nordic Council, K.-A. Fagerholm, characterized the agreement as follows: "It was watered down, it was altogether too general, it was not binding, etc. All this is true and correct. But just as true, the best is often the enemy of the good. We can be fairly content with the Helsinki Agreement. . . ."[25]

The governments of Finland and Sweden were pleased with the agreement because of the message of Nordic unity which it might convey to the rest of Europe, during the consideration of neutral European Free Trade Association members' applications for admission to the European Economic Community.[26] The government of Denmark made advance inquiries in Brussels and ascertained that the Helsinki Agreement would not prejudice the Danish application for membership in the EEC.

The Treaty of Cooperation between Denmark, Finland, Iceland, Norway, and Sweden entered into force on July 1, 1962. It recorded past successes in Scandinavian cooperation and exhorted their extension. But it did not alter the status of the Nordic Council as an interparliamentary organ of consultation. Article 36 of the Helsinki Agreement merely states that the Council "should be

[24] The Helsinki Agreement is found in Appendix D. See Stanley V. Anderson, "The Nordic Council and the 1962 Helsinki Agreement," *Nordisk Tidsskrift for International Ret*, XXXIV, No. 4 (1964), 278–300.

[25] "Tionde sessionen," *Nordisk Kontakt*, No. 6 (1962), p. 302.

[26] See John Boyens, "Integrationsprobleme für Schweden und Finnland," *Aussenpolitik*, XIV, No. 6 (June, 1963), 407.

given an opportunity to express its views on questions of Nordic cooperation that are of importance in principle, whenever this is not impossible due to lack of time." By enumerating accomplishments and listing goals, the treaty has identified these matters as official government policy in the five states. This identification should prove useful to the Secretaries-General in reminding civil servants in the national bureaucracies of their Nordic responsibilities.

The leaders of the Nordic Council will no doubt continue to press for increased domestic political influence in the four larger countries. The conclusion remains that, after a dozen years of operation, the Council has not succeeded in systematic penetration of the governments, either as an external pressure group or as an integral part of government. The level of intergovernmental cooperation is high, but the executive chooses the topics and sets the pace. The governments believe that the bulk of inter-Scandinavian activity must remain on the governmental plane, and that the main task of the Council is "to mold opinion, to try to engage our countrymen, to interest them, to make them enthusiastic, as far as possible, over the ideas [put forward] in the Nordic Council." [27]

[27] Remarks of the Swedish Prime Minister, Tage Erlander, in general debate at the eighth session of the Nordic Council, *1960 Record,* p. 56.

Chapter Six

COMMON NORDIC

MARKET NEGOTIATIONS

Scandinavian regionalism provides an opportunity for study of early stages in the process of community formation. The Nordic countries have been twice on the verge of integration since the end of World War II. On neither occasion did they cross the threshold. The first flirtation with union was the 1948–49 proposal for a Scandinavian Defense Alliance, discussed in Chapter 2. The second approach to amalgamation was in the economic sphere, and stretched from 1947 to 1959.

The Foreign Ministers of Denmark, Iceland, Norway, and Sweden met in July, 1947, and the Norwegian Minister proposed the establishment of a special committee to investigate means toward further development of economic cooperation in Scandinavia. In February of 1948, these ministers set up the Joint Nordic Committee for Economic Cooperation (hereinafter referred to as the "1948 Committee"), described in Chapter 5. The experts on the 1948 Committee were given the task of investigating the possibilities of (a) establishing a common external Northern tariff as a preliminary step toward a customs union; (b) reducing inter-Scandinavian tariffs and quantitative restrictions; (c) increasing division of labor and specialization in Scandinavia, in cooperation with appropriate private organizations; and (d) expanding previous Nordic commercial cooperation.

The 1948 Committee made a fifty-page preliminary report to the governments of Denmark, Iceland, Norway, and Sweden in January, 1950.[1] The report itself was unanimous: it asserted that a customs union of the four countries would bring mutual advantage through larger-scale production resulting from a enlarged population base of approximately fourteen million persons. It would also make the countries more competitive internationally. A ten-year transition period was discussed, to cushion anticipated difficulties. However, it was also noted that a customs union would entail special problems for Norway, whose spotty industrialization would have to be filled out before such a union would be profitable. The Norwegian reservations and Iceland's status as an observer led the 1948 Committee to conclude that it was not possible at that time to carry out a customs union among the four countries.

Nevertheless, cabinet ministers from the several countries met in November, 1950, and all agreed that further negotiations with Norway were preferable to a separate Dano-Swedish customs union. The government directed the 1948 Committee to investigate the fundamental and technical preconditions for the elimination of customs duties between the Scandinavian countries for certain segments of the economies or for certain types of commodities. As before, the 1948 Committee made use of prominent persons within the industries being studied, in proceeding with this more limited task.

At the first annual session of the Nordic Council (February, 1953), there was a short debate on economic cooperation based on an incomplete report from the 1948 Committee. Recommendation 5/1953 asserted that closer economic cooperation between the countries had possibilities of strengthening their respective economies, but that complicated problems were involved which required intensive investigation to ensure that each country would find cooperation advantageous. Thus, the Council requested the governments to instruct the 1948 Committee to complete its investigations as soon as possible, and to submit its report to the governments with a statement of conclusions. The Council next noted that the 1948 Committee's investigations of particular industries had shown that cooperation among some of them would result in immediate mutual benefit, and the recommendation concluded by requesting the governments to present the forthcoming report of the 1948 Committee to the Council to permit the issue to be

[1] *Nordisk økonomisk samarbejde* (Copenhagen: Jørgensen, 1950).

discussed at the next session. The governments instructed the 1948 Committee to submit its report in the spring of 1954.

This report was made public on May 31, 1954.[2] It covered twenty-one branches of industry. The Danish and Swedish members of the committee concluded that all of these could profit through the gradual institution of respective common markets, but that the change-over should be made branch by branch, after negotiation with GATT, beginning with the most promising industries, as follows: furniture, heavy chemicals, paint and varnish, porcelain, leather and shoes, textiles, agricultural and tool-making machinery, and radio manufacture. The Norwegian members concluded that Norwegian industry needed protection in most of these fields, while in those branches where Norwegian industrialists had expressed a desire to have a common market, the Swedes and Danes were reluctant, such as fish canning, aluminum semimanufactures, and certain iron alloy manufactures. The 1948 Committee noted that agricultural and trade union organizations had generally given support to the idea of an industrial common market. The Swedish and Danish members recommended that the governments of Denmark, Norway, and Sweden undertake concrete negotiations toward instituting a common market in the twenty-one industries covered in the report. Iceland did not take part in the investigation of the twenty-one industries, and the Icelandic observer did not participate in a majority of the meetings of the 1948 Committee. Thus, the report does not embrace Iceland. The Norwegian government later published a commentary on the report,[3] in which the Norwegian position was restated and alternative areas of cooperation—other than a common market—were suggested.

At the second session of the Nordic Council (August, 1954), the common market issue was considered thoroughly by the Standing Committee on Economic Matters. A minority of the committee, consisting of one Norwegian Conservative delegate and one Norwegian Liberal delegate, wanted the matter postponed to the next session, but the majority wanted immediate submission of the issue

---

[2] *En gemensam Nordisk marknad* (Stockholm: Statens Offentliga Utredningar, No. 13, 1954), also printed in Danish (Copenhagen: Schultz, 1954) and Norwegian (Trondheim: Sentrum, 1954).

[3] *Utredning om et nærmere økonomiske samarbeid i Norden* (Oslo: Ministry of Commerce, 1954).

to the plenary body. The majority asserted that a common market could be instituted by using different methods and speeds in the various industries and in the several countries, and that preparations were so far advanced as to warrant the governments to take charge. The Danish and Swedish delegates were seemingly ready to recommend immediate steps for a Swedish-Danish common market until it appeared that the Norwegian Labor party, which was in power in Norway, supported the Danes and Swedes "in principle." After lengthy debate, the majority's position was accepted in session by a vote of forty-three to zero, including all the votes of the Norwegian Labor party delegates, but with eight other Norwegians abstaining. The result was the Nordic Council's Recommendation 22/1954, as follows:

> The Nordic Council recommends that the Governments promote closer economic cooperation between the Nordic countries.
> Specifically, the Council recommends,
> 1. that the Governments seek to prepare the ground for the establishment of as comprehensive a common Nordic market as possible;
> 2. that, on the basis of the data submitted by the [1948] Committee . . . , the Governments clarify the possibilities of applying uniform tariff rates (or restrictions) vis-à-vis non-Nordic countries and initiate endeavors to abolish intra-Nordic customs duties and trade restrictions to the extent and at the rate considered to be compatible with the special conditions of each country;
> 3. that the Governments initiate negotiations concerning cooperation in specific fields which have important bearings on the productivity and the living standards of the Nordic countries . . . ;
> 4. that the Governments charge a responsible body with the task of promoting and supervising this work in accordance with the above directives.[4]

In October of 1954 there was a meeting of members of the governments of Denmark, Norway, and Sweden, headed by their Prime Ministers. This group appointed a committee of Ministers of Economic Cooperation (hereinafter referred to as the "Ministerial Committee"), consisting of one cabinet member from each country, and a Nordic Economic Cooperation Committee (hereinafter referred to as the "NECC"), whose make-up was described in Chapter 5. Guiding principles for both committees were stated as follows:

[4] Translated in the introduction to *Nordic Economic Cooperation* (Copenhagen: Schultz, 1958), pp. 11–12. See note 9, below.

The work shall aim primarily at the following objectives:

1. To map out . . . intra-Nordic trade with a view to determining in what commodity sectors conditions exist for rapid establishment of a common market in fields where customs duties and quantitative restrictions are of minor significance. In addition, it should be determined in what other sectors the introduction of a common market could be expected to involve more advantages than drawbacks for the three countries. . . .

2. To examine whether there are sectors of production where an expansion could advantageously be carried out through a joint Nordic effort or where coordination is desirable.

3. To clarify the necessary assumptions under which a common Nordic market will be compatible with the efforts to expand trade with countries outside the Nordic area and with the obligations arising out of membership in international organizations.

4. To examine the conditions which influence the relative competitive ability of the industries of the three countries (subsidies, wage, interest and tax levels, including tax-free depreciation).

5. To prepare a uniform customs nomenclature on the basis of the Brussels Nomenclature, and also a uniform nomenclature for trade statistics.

In principle, the work should be organized on the following lines:

a. The Government of each country shall appoint a Minister who will be responsible for the preparation of matters concerning Nordic economic cooperation. The three ministers will jointly consider how such matters shall be handled.

b. A Nordic [Economic] Cooperation Committee consisting of three representatives of each country shall be established. This Committee will, either by itself or by means of experts, conduct further studies [and will]

c. . . . constitute a body for coordination of internal administrative work on Nordic economic questions. . . . It is to function in close contact with the organizations of industry, business, agriculture and labor.[5]

The common market was only briefly discussed at the third session of the Nordic Council (January, 1955). The report of the NECC was not scheduled to be finished until later in the year. The Council expressed its hope that specific proposals could be made at the next session, one year later.

The NECC published a fifty-page report in June, 1955,[6] a technical and statistical study which—as stated in the foreword—made no attempt at evaluation nor proposal for implementation.

The Presidium of the Nordic Council met in October, 1955,

[5] Translated in *Nordic Economic Cooperation*, pp. 12–13.
[6] *Nordisk samhandel* (Copenhagen: Nielsen and Lydiche, 1955).

together with members of the governments of Denmark, Iceland, Norway, and Sweden, including the Prime Ministers of all but Iceland, and asked the Ministerial Committee to submit a progress report to the fourth annual session of the Nordic Council in January, 1956.

At this session, the Council received the NECC report,[7] and a report from the governments on the NECC's work. Some general debate ensued before the matter was referred to the Council's Standing Committee on Economic Matters. After intensive debate, this committee unanimously proposed that the studies continue. As to the motivation for the proposal, however, there was disagreement. Two of the Norwegian committee members, one Liberal and one Conservative, did not object to the continuation of the investigations, but felt that it had so far been shown that a common Nordic market would on the whole be disadvantageous for Norway. The majority proposed only that the studies be continued, rather than asking for specific implementation, because the studies were not complete. Two days of debate in plenary session followed. The idea of a common Nordic market was opposed by non-Labor Norwegian delegates, while all others supported it. No new recommendation ensued, but the work of the Ministerial Committee and of the NECC was approved, and these bodies were then to continue their work under prior instructions. Further treatment of the common market was to await new communications from the governments at a later session.

The fourth session saw Finland participating for the first time. Finland encouraged the other nations to continue their investigations and favored the idea of a common market, but Finnish spokesmen noted that Finland could not yet join one. Icelandic representatives expressed interest in the work and a desire to follow developments with the idea of eventually joining, but stated that Iceland could not at that time take part in a common market. In August of 1956, Finland added representatives to the Ministerial Committee and to the NECC and began participation in investigations on Scandinavian economic cooperation. Previous studies of branches of industry were to be supplemented to include Finland.

At the fifth session of the Nordic Council (February, 1957), the Economic Matters Committee noted that Finland was now on a

[7] *Beretning om nordisk økonomisk samarbejde*, Item C 5/1956 on the Nordic Council sessional agenda.

parity with the other countries in the investigation of its industries by the NECC. It further noted that the report of the NECC would be ready in July, 1957, and that this report would throw light on the Northern countries' relations to the proposed West European free trade area. The committee proposed that no new recommendation be made until the next session. A single day's debate followed in plenary session, with the Swedish, Finnish, and Danish delegates and the Norwegian Laborites arguing that broader European plans did not lessen the value of a Northern common market, while the other Norwegian delegates argued that the latter was no longer a significant factor in the face of the larger free trade area. The Economic Committee's proposal was unanimously adopted.

All the research of previous years culminated in October, 1957, when the NECC submitted its report to the Ministerial Committee.[8] The report was in five volumes: the first was a general part, outlining a plan for a common Nordic market to include 80 per cent of current intra-Scandinavian trade;[9] the second discussed particular branches of industry;[10] the third volume covered some special problems of cooperation;[11] the fourth proposed a common schedule of tariffs and transitional measures;[12] and, the last volume presented a common nomenclature for trade statistics.[13]

[8] *Nordisk økonomisk samarbeid* (Vols. I–IV, Oslo: Gundersen, 1957; Vol. V, Stockholm: Norstedt, 1957).

[9] *Generell Del: Plan for et utvidet økonomiske samarbeide.* This volume covered the organizational and institutional aspects of the plan, and it has been translated into English as *Nordic Economic Cooperation.* The draft convention on Nordic economic cooperation and the draft agreement for the Nordic Investment Bank are included.

[10] *Speciell Del: Vareomraadene.* The groups covered are as follows: wood and wood products, iron and steel, metals and metal products, machinery, electrical equipment and transport equipment, chemicals, pharmaceutical products, and "other commodities."

[11] *Speciell Del: Økonomiske samarbeidsproblemer.* This volume proposed to ensure fair terms of competition with reference to excise taxes, price controls, cartels, and monopolies, to establish appropriate finance and foreign exchange measures, and to provide for cooperation in research, education, anti-dumping measures, and rules of customs administration.

[12] This volume consists of two appendices: *Bilag I: Forslag til felles tolltariff,* and *Bilag II: Forslag til overgangsordninger.* These are detailed proposed schedules of tariffs and progressive reductions or equalizations thereof.

[13] This volume is also an appendix: *Bilag III: Statistisk samarbete.* Steps have since been taken in the national parliaments to institute a common terminology based, where appropriate, on the Brussels nomenclature.

The proposed common Nordic market would have had a Council of Ministers for a governing body, with voting on the principle of unanimity.

Later in October, 1957, the Ministerial Committee convened to consider the relationship between the Nordic market and the European free trade area. The November meeting of the Nordic Council's Standing Committee on Economic Matters was attended by members of the Council's Presidium, representatives of those parties in Denmark, Finland, Norway, and Sweden not having seats on the Economic Committee, the Ministerial Committee, and a majority of the members of the NECC. There was general agreement that Scandinavia should encourage the European free trade area and should help Danish agriculture find an acceptable place within it. The 1957 report of the NECC was not discussed in detail (the appendices not yet being available), but the basic issues of a common Nordic market were debated. Discussion was predicated on the assumption that both the all-West European free trade area and the Inner-Six's European Economic Community (EEC) would soon be realized. It was argued that Scandinavian plans were more extensive than were those of the free trade area, and that the North would have a stronger position within the area if it were able to bargain as a unit. Furthermore, the participation of Finland might be made possible if there were a pre-existing Nordic customs union. The Norwegian bourgeois parties argued that each nation would be better able to bargain if unfettered and that a Nordic customs union would be of questionable value within a European free trade area. No final positions on a common Nordic market were taken.

In the 1957 report of the NECC, it was stated that a supplementary report would be prepared on the effect of West European cooperation on the North. The NECC also expected to add to its study the 20 per cent of intra-Nordic trade which had not been covered in the 1957 report. In November, 1957, the Presidium of the Nordic Council met and recommended postponement of the 1958 meeting of the Council to permit this supplementary information to be presented to the session. The Presidium also expressed its willingness to call another interim meeting of the expanded Economic Matters Committee before the rescheduled 1958 session.

Such an interim meeting was arranged in September, 1958. The report on the last 20 per cent of intra-Nordic trade—goods generally protected by higher tariffs than those of the earlier 80 per cent—was submitted and discussed.[14] The preparatory studies of the NECC were now considered to be complete. But the group was to continue its research on the position of agriculture and to proceed with its studies of the mutual impact of Scandinavian and West European economic integration. The Economic Matters Committee stated that a common Nordic market would increase Scandinavian productivity and would strengthen bargaining power, particularly in free trade area negotiations. It was felt that the several Scandinavian governments could not be expected to take a stand on a Northern customs union until the future of the West European free trade area was more predictable; willingness to call an extraordinary session of the Council was expressed.

The sixth session of the Nordic Council finally convened in November, 1958, with Norway as the host nation. The question of economic cooperation dominated debate, erupting at the opening meeting before the matter was referred to the Economic Matters Committee. Prime Minister Tage Erlander of Sweden urged that the governments make positive and prompt political decisions on a common Nordic market. The Finnish Prime Minister, Karl-August Fagerholm, skirted the customs union issue by emphasizing that Finland would condition its participation in Northern economic integration on the common market's ability to increase trade with Eastern Europe (which effect Erlander insisted it could have). The acting Danish Prime Minister, Viggo Kampmann, subordinated his approval of a common Nordic market to his concern with the prompt institution of the broader West European free trade area—he hoped that successful negotiations for the latter would soon permit a favorable decision to be made within Scandinavia. Prime Minister Einar Gerhardsen of Norway first reminded the Council that his government had not yet taken a stand on a Scandinavian customs union, then reviewed the difficulties which Norwegian industry might encounter.

[14] Together with the earlier NECC reports, the supplementary reports—comprising an additional five hundred pages—were printed as a second volume of the official record of the sixth annual session of the Nordic Council: *Nordisk Råd: 6. sesjon, 1958*. Volume II of the *1958 Record* contains 1,854 pages. The general part of the 1958 supplementary report of the NECC has been translated into English as *Nordic Economic Cooperation: Supplementary Report* (Copenhagen: Schultz, 1959).

After four days' deliberation, the Economic Matters Standing Committee unanimously presented its committee proposals, later adopted by the Council as Recommendations 26/1958 and 27/1958, as follows:

> The Nordic Council recommends that the Governments of Denmark, Finland, Norway and Sweden commence negotiations, based on [prior] reports and in contact with the Council, on the forms of Nordic economic cooperation, with a view to presenting the matter to the Parliaments when the preconditions for a decision are present.
>
> The Council recommends that the Governments advise their representatives in the OEEC of the above views, and direct them to do their utmost together in OEEC negotiations to foster a solution which will assure the establishment and strengthening of economic cooperation in Europe through the creation of a free trade area.

Finnish representatives abstained from all voting on Recommendation 27/1958, Finland not being a member of the Organization for European Economic Cooperation. Immediately after taking action on November 13, 1958, the Standing Committee on Economic Matters sent telegrams to Paris to inform Scandinavian delegates there of the content of the proposed recommendations. The cabinet members to whom telegrams were sent had participated earlier in the standing committee's deliberations on the recommendations. On November 14, 1958, Arne Skaug, Norwegian Minister of Commerce, reported to the OEEC free trade area conference ministers on behalf of the governments of Denmark, Iceland, Norway, and Sweden, and informed them of the proceedings and proposals of the Nordic Council committee.

Council debate on the recommendations showed no basic shifts in position. There was more emphasis on Northern unity as an important factor in the West European free trade area negotiations, but less emphasis on a customs union as the only possible form for joint action to take. The Swedes were relatively more outspoken in their desire for a common Nordic market as an economic value in itself. The same non-Labor Norwegian delegates had the same doubts as before. Iceland was still unable to participate in economic integration because fish products were her sole important exportable commodity.

Except for one Icelandic vote, the recommendations were accepted unanimously on November 14, 1958. This was possible because there was no recommendation as to what position the governments should take, but only that they should eventually take some position.

The OEEC conference in Paris was unsuccessful, and the initial EEC tariff reductions came into effect on January 1, 1959, without *rapprochement* between the EEC Inner-Six (Belgium, France, Holland, Italy, Luxemburg, and West Germany) and the Outer-Seven (Austria, Britain, Denmark, Norway, Portugal, Sweden, and Switzerland). At first, the outsiders tried to reopen negotiations for a thirteen-nation free trade area, but gradually turned instead to the formation of a separate seven-nation European Free Trade Association (EFTA).

The common Nordic market was shelved somewhere in the course of EFTA negotiations in June and July of 1959. The non-Scandinavian members of EFTA might have accepted an already going Nordic customs union, but they saw no need for creating one within the Outer-Seven. Crucial in the abandonment of Nordic market proposals was the vacillation of the Scandinavian governments, as expressed at the 1958 session of the Nordic Council.

In the middle of July, 1959, when the Finnish government presented an official confirmation of Finland's readiness to enter a common Nordic market, the governments of Denmark, Norway, and Sweden were unable to reciprocate. EFTA negotiations proceeded rapidly, spurred by the desire to face the EEC with a united front, and the Outer-Seven governments agreed upon the formation of the European Free Trade Association at a conference in Stockholm on July 20–21, 1959. "This, in fact, sealed the doom of the Northern Customs Union." [15]

A second supplementary report of the NECC, nearly 200 pages in length, was presented at the 1959 session of the Nordic Council as Item D 63/1959, but it was clearly anticlimactic. Other events which followed the abandonment of the common Nordic market plans—the heated debates at the 1959 session, the creation of a new Nordic Ministerial Committee for Economic Cooperation, the reorganization of the NECC, the Harpsund meeting in October, 1960—were related in Chapter 5.

[15] Arthur Montgomery, "From a Northern Customs Union to EFTA," *Scandinavian Economic History Review*, VIII, No. 1 (1960), 67.

The national policies toward Scandinavian regionalism which were delineated in the introduction are plainly reflected in the common Nordic market negotiations. The role of the Nordic Council as a sounding board of parliamentary and public opinion on basic issues of inter-Scandinavian relations, as described in Chapter 2, is also confirmed. The dominance of the Council's Presidium and secretariat in carrying out this role, as put forward in Chapter 3, is consistent with the history of these negotiations, while the tendency toward bland unanimity portrayed in Chapter 4 is clearly illustrated in the series of recommendations on Nordic economic cooperation which emerged from the Council's annual sessions.

Finally, the identification, made in Chapter 5, of the executive as the real decision maker and fact finder in matters of Scandinavian integration and cooperation is distinctly reinforced. The governments took the more direct responsibility for establishing and instructing the investigatory bodies, replicating the parliamentary relationship between cabinet and legislature in the several states. Because positive political agreement could not be reached by the governments, progress was limited to technical matters, such as nomenclature and statistics. On basic questions, the governments could only agree that a final answer should not be recorded.

Three factors to be described in the concluding chapter operated to prolong negotiations as long as any elite group wished them to continue: (1) renunciation of the use of force as an arbiter of disputes; (2) feelings of mutual sympathy (continuing the venerable Pan-Scandinavian movement); and (3) great increase in communication between corresponding social and economic groups, already sketched in its governmental aspect in Chapter 5. Material bonuses, such as the Nordic Investment Bank, which would have provided Swedish capital for use in Norway, were not sufficient to overcome economic nationalism.

Temporizing took the form of referring the issue back to the experts for more information. Investigation became a substitute for integration. As Danish Foreign Minister, Per Hækkerup noted:

> Our approach was to ask experts to determine and describe the difficulties that had to be overcome before such a customs union could be formed. No stone was left unturned, no question unanswered. The outcome of concentrated work in the Nordic Council was thirteen thousand pages of arguments for and against a customs union. But while we were discussing and elaborating these problems

from every conceivable angle, developments in Europe passed us by.[16]

By way of contrast, the political decision to form a Benelux customs union was made in advance of technical studies; the experts there were asked to arrange the implementation of the decision rather than to evaluate its feasibility. The former chairman of the Norwegian section of the NECC argues that:

> The Nordic countries ought to . . . prevent their foreign economic policy from becoming a one-sided accommodation to situations which are created for them by other countries. They ought to be willing to make political decisions in this area without always demanding comprehensive and detailed study beforehand. The Six made the political decisions first, and then asked the experts for help in carrying them out.[17]

Scandinavian economic integration has now been sublimated into continental dimensions. Reflecting the characteristic Scandinavian emphasis on practical ends rather than on integration for its own sake, key political leaders have accepted economic integration as a practicable political program, but have concluded that expectations of increased national product, with continued full employment, can best be met on a European basis rather than on a Nordic one.

An exclusive common Nordic market might still be realized if economic warfare within Western Europe were to threaten the broadly based high standard of living of the Scandinavian countries, whose leaders might then be forced to accept, *faute de mieux,* the Northern population base of twenty million persons as a minimal economic unit. This would be a dubious victory for Nordic integration, inasmuch as it presumes the fragmentation of Western Europe.

Proposals for a common Nordic market within EFTA were made in Copenhagen at the 1966 session of the Nordic Council. Positive action was thwarted by Danish reluctance to complicate

[16] Per Hækkerup, "Nordic Co-operation and the World Around Us," an address given to the annual meeting of the Danish Norden Association on June 13, 1964 (mimeographed by the Danish Nordic Council secretariat), p. 4.

[17] Knut Getz Wold, "Norge, Norden og markedsproblemene," *Nordisk Kontakt,* No. 10 (1963), p. 581.

possible adherence to the 1957 Treaty of Rome which established the EEC.

A lengthy and complex proposal was negotiated in the Economic Matters Committee, and adopted unanimously as Recommendation 26/1966. The upshot was to ask the governments to study the matter. In an incisive article, Nils Lundgren analyzes the situation as follows:

> After free intra-Nordic trade in industrial goods has been achieved through EFTA the remaining problems are mainly political. . . . The decision at the Nordic Council session in February 1966 to refer the question to study by the Economic Commission therefore seems particularly inappropriate unless it is a way of giving up without saying so publicly.[18]

The failure to conclude a common Nordic market should not be allowed to becloud the success of Scandinavian economic integration in other forms, dating back to the 1946 consortium of Danish, Norwegian, and Swedish airlines to form the Scandinavian Airlines System (SAS). In a striking recent innovation, Denmark, Finland, Norway, and Sweden are negotiating as a unit, with a single spokesman, in the Kennedy Round of tariff reductions under GATT. In protracted deliberations in Geneva, the members of GATT are working for substantial across-the-board cuts in customs duties, so that EEC and EFTA will not become protectionist islands.

Finnish association with EFTA on June 26, 1961, brought the last of the four larger Scandinavian countries into a hundred-million-person free trade area. By the middle of 1965, tariffs on most industrial goods within EFTA had been reduced by 70 per cent. For the most part, residual quotas were lifted and remaining tariffs eliminated at the end of 1966. This represents an acceleration of three years over the original timetable.

The impact of the European Free Trade Area upon Scandinavia has been remarkable. According to the *EFTA Reporter:*

> In the five years following the signing of the Stockholm Convention, the Scandinavian countries' trade with one another increased by 110%—or more than twice as much as the previous years.
>
> This impressive rise must be seen in the light of the fact that over

[18] Nils Lundgren, "Nordic Common Market—For and Against," *EFTA Bulletin,* VII, No. 3 (April, 1966), 15.

the same five years, 1960–64, the Scandinavian countries increased their exports to all EFTA countries by 78% and to the world as a whole by 60%.[19]

The common Nordic labor market is also a significant achievement, even though it has not resulted in a mass exchange of workers. Sweden is by far the largest importer of neighboring Scandinavian labor. In 1964, there were nearly one hundred thousand workers from Denmark, Finland, and Norway living in Sweden. More than sixty-five thousand of these were Finns, while the Norwegians and Danes accounted for roughly eighteen thousand and twelve thousand respectively.[20] At the same time, there were about eight thousand Danes and Swedes, plus a few hundred Finns, working and living in Norway.[21] Danish and Finnish importation of workers is in the same range as the Norwegian.

In contrast to compact, homogeneous Scandinavia, the EFTA countries are divided by language, religion, and geography. Why did the Nordic nations choose to enter this conglomeration, and yet refuse to form a separate Northern customs union? From the trade statistics given in the introductory chapter, it is clear that the northern corner of Europe could not afford to be excluded from the markets to the south. Intra-Nordic markets were smaller and less vulnerable (representing about one fifth of total foreign trade). In the absence of compelling economic reasons for Nordic union, the countries were free to give rein to the prevailing national sentiments, as analyzed in the next chapter.

[19] "EFTA's Merging Scandinavian Markets," *EFTA Reporter*, No. 118 (April 26, 1965), p. 4.

[20] See *Nytt från Nordiska rådet*, No. 5 (May 20, 1965), p. 71.

[21] *Ibid.*, p. 75.

Chapter Seven

CONCLUSION

The political history of Northern Europe since the Kalmar Union (1397–*ca.* 1523) has been one of fragmentation: Sweden-Finland withdrew fitfully from the Union in the fifteenth and early sixteenth centuries; Norway attained internal independence with separation from Denmark in 1814, and her subsequent union with Sweden was dissolved in 1905; after centuries as an integral part of the Swedish kingdom, Finland became an autonomous Duchy of the Russian Czar in 1809, and won complete independence in 1917–18; Iceland gained independence in 1918, and terminated her union with Denmark in 1944. Norway, Finland, and Iceland, then, did not become full-fledged nation-states until the present century.

The splintering process has now stopped. None of the Scandinavian countries is plagued by disruptive separatist movements. There are no outstanding territorial disputes and no fortified boundaries. Only a few residues of incomplete assimilation persevere.

Swede-Finns are the largest cultural minority in Scandinavia, comprising about 7.5 per cent of the population of Finland, concentrated in the coastal districts to the south and west. Communities become officially bilingual whenever the minority group, whether Swedish or Finnish, makes up 10 per cent of local population. Because the Swedish population is proportionally diminishing, this rule was liberalized in 1962 to provide that a community would stay bilingual even if the minority fell below

8 per cent, as long as at least five thousand members remained in it.[1]

The nearly twenty-two thousand Swede-Finns who inhabit the Åland Islands have a special status, enjoying local autonomy in addition to the general constitutional guarantees of cultural integrity. The decision by the League of Nations in 1920 that the islands belong to Finland was accepted by both Finland and Sweden. At the same time, Finland was held to be bound by the Treaty of Peace of 1856, under which Russia had promised not to fortify them. Finally, the League provided guarantees of home rule, in recognition of the Swedish sentiments of the Ålanders—sentiments which still prevail.

With twelve seats out of two hundred in the Finnish Parliament, the Swedish People's party fosters Scandinavian and especially Swedish-Finnish ties. Swede-Finns are conscious of their identity, but work for self-perpetuation within the Finnish state. Their primary loyalty is to Finland.

Other nationalities are quite small. Denmark has three of them. Some thirty-three thousand Faeroese have local home rule under the Danish crown. Fewer then half favor complete independence. For several years, starting in 1958, Johan Poulsen attended the Nordic Council as an elected member from the Danish Moderate Liberal party. His successor in the Danish Parliament, Peter Mohr Dam, attended the 1965 session as an alternate Social Democratic member, but boycotted the 1966 session and refused election to the 1967 delegation, in protest against exclusion of the Faeroese flag in Nordic Council ceremonies. Both the Faeroe Island and the Åland Island legislatures would like to be directly represented in the Council. The question of Faeroese representation will be taken up at the 1967 session.

Greenland also has two delegates in the Danish Parliament. With a native population of approximately twenty-five thousand, the world's largest island was made an integral part of the Danish kingdom under the 1953 Constitution, and thereby ceased technically to be a colony.

[1] See Klaus Törnudd, "The Language Situation in Finland," *American-Scandinavian Review*, LI No. 1 (March, 1963), 27–32, and V. Merikoski, "The Realization of the Equality of the National Languages in Finland," in *Democracy in Finland* (Helsinki: Finnish Political Science Association, 1960), pp. 81–92.

The Schleswig party represents the German minority in Denmark. Until 1964, the nine thousand votes which the party marshals in national elections were enough to return a member to Parliament. In that year, however, the party lost its lone parliamentary representative.

In the far north of Scandinavia, the Lapps are divided among three countries—twenty-five hundred in Finland, ten thousand in Sweden, and twenty thousand in Norway—but there is no agitation for political autonomy. (Another fifteen hundred to two thousand Lapps live in the Soviet Union.)

Self-determination of peoples has been carried just about as far as it can go. The internal homogeneity of each Nordic country is recapitulated in diluted form among the countries taken as a whole. The five nations share ties of geography, language, race, religion, trade, political organization, and history. Many of these cross contacts are institutionalized in voluntary associations: nongovernmental inter-Scandinavian organizations are legion.[2]

Strong secondary loyalties to Scandinavia as a whole exist among some segments of the populations. They have their modern origins in the Pan-Scandinavian movement of the 1840's to 1860's, and have been given most consistent expression in this century by the semiofficial Norden Societies, which were founded in 1919 in Denmark, Norway, and Sweden. With the addition of branches in Iceland (1922), Finland (1924), and the Faeroe Islands (1951), there are now six separately organized societies, each with its own national bureau. There was no central secretariat until 1965, when the Union of Norden Societies was established.

In 1957, total Norden Society membership was about 120,000, divided as follows: Denmark, 60,000 members; Sweden, 25,000; Finland, 21,000; Norway, 12,000; Iceland, 1,300; and the Faeroe Islands, 600.[3] The number of members provides a rough index of

[2] A sampling is provided by Raymond E. Lindgren, "International Cooperation in Scandinavia," *Year Book of World Affairs*, XIII, (1959), 97. A chronology of Nordic events is included in each issue of *Nordisk Tidskrift*, in the section entitled "Norden." The more prominent activities are described in "The Quarter's History" of *The American-Scandinavian Review*.

[3] *Protokol over forhandlingerne ved foreningerne Nordens delegeretmøde, 1957*, p. 63. By 1958, Icelandic membership had increased to 2,000; see *Protokoll över förhandlingarna vid föreningarna Nordens delegerademöte, 1958*, p. 5. Compare *Pohjola-Norden Verksamhetsberättelse för år 1959*, p. 2, which gives the following membership figures: Denmark, 60,000; Sweden,

identification with Scandinavia in each country. Leaders of the Norden Societies attend meetings of the Nordic Council and the Nordic Cultural Commission as officially invited guests or experts.

The populations at large tend more and more to work, travel, and play in one another's countries. They have a generally permissive attitude toward international cooperation, and are favorably disposed to Nordic cooperation—for its own sake, for its practical usefulness, and as an example to the rest of the world.

Might not these attitudes and associations permit the growth of a federalism-from-below, a knitting together of the economies, cultures, and governments which would increase until union need only be recognized as a *fait accompli?* Cultural affinities are sometimes cited as a basis for integration. F. S. C. Northrop asserts that integration "will not be effective unless there are common norms in the living law corresponding to and supporting the [new supranational norms]." [4] History demonstrates that common heritage is neither a necessary condition (Canada, Switzerland, Yugoslavia) nor a sufficient condition (Scandinavia, the Arab world, Latin America) for amalgamation. Like peoples can unite or separate, and disparate peoples can effect political union if they want to. Mutual tolerance can be institutionalized to fit any of these permutations. The variety of possible political arrangements is unlimited.

The volitional nature of amalgamation is revealed in the following description of the first essential condition for the formation of a "security-community:" ". . . a compatibility of the main values held by the politically relevant strata of all participating units [s]ometimes . . . supplemented by a tacit agreement to deprive of political significance any incompatible values that might remain." [5]

The peoples of Scandinavia do not want to merge. Primary loyalty is firmly lodged in the nation-state. [6] National separatism

---

30,000; Finland, 16,000; Norway, 11,000; Iceland, 2,000; the Faeroe Islands, 600.

[4] F. S. C. Northrop, *European Union and United States Foreign Policy* (New York: Macmillan, 1954), p. 31.

[5] Karl W. Deutsch *et al., Political Community and the North Atlantic Area* (Princeton, N.J.: Princeton University Press, 1957), p. 46. The members of a security-community settle their disputes without violence (see footnote 11, below). The authors assume that the same conditions are relevant to amalgamation.

[6] See Otto L. Karlstrom, "The 'Scandinavian' Approach to Political Integration" (Ph.D. dissertation, University of Chicago, 1952). The predomi-

has triumphed whenever challenged—e.g., in the breakdown of Defense Alliance negotiations in 1949, in the abandonment of the proposal for a common Nordic market in 1959, in the repeated emasculation of programs for political integration, and, more recently, in the attempted *sauve qui peux* switch from EFTA to common market.

The consciousness of distinguishing characteristics, real or imaginary, is stronger than the sense of shared values. Each national group applies the principle of "narcissism in respect of minor differences" which Sigmund Freud ascribed to nations.[7] These differences are taken as marks of superiority, although they are expressed for reasons of modesty in terms of the inferiority of the outsider. That one's neighbors are too forward (or too reserved), too foolhardy (or too pusillanimous), too condescending (or too deferential), is a matter of general knowledge in each of the countries, firmly inculcated and able to withstand any number of individual exceptions. These attitudes would not necessarily prevent political integration—similar invidious comparisons are made by neighbors within a given nation—but they certainly do not foster it.

Once dominant, mutual exclusion tends to gain momentum. Gunnar Myrdal argues that national boundaries result in a closed circuit which is self-perpetuating:

> . . . the entire social development during the last two or three generations in Scandinavia has increased immensely the interest ties of every single individual to the community on his side of the boundary. And, on balance, this probably counts more than the very intensive conscious efforts which have gone on in Scandinavia to strengthen the ties between the countries, for instance in the fields of civil and social legislation.[8]

---

nance of nationalism within Scandinavia is the burden of this thesis, emerging from an historical study of the disparity "Between the popular usage of the Scandinavian term and its real political importance . . ." (p. 6).

[7] Sigmund Freud, *Civilization and Its Discontents* (Garden City, N.Y.: Doubleday Anchor, n.d.), pp. 64–65. See Herbert Hendin, *Suicide and Scandinavia* (New York: Grune and Stratton, 1964; Garden City, N.Y.: Doubleday Anchor, 1965), for a profound study of what is distinctive in Danish, Norwegian, and Swedish national character.

[8] Gunnar Myrdal, *Psychological Impediments to Effective International Cooperation* (New York: Journal of Social Issues Supplement Series, No. 6, 1952), p. 19.

Political disunity leads to and is reinforced by economic fragmentation. W. R. Mead asserts that there "may be tendencies towards
functional unity between the five countries, but the separate economies as outlined by existing political boundaries are the real functional units." [9]

Increased contact between individual Scandinavians and the
proliferation of inter-Scandinavian organizations have not altered
basic loyalties. Casual or impersonal cross-national contact is as
likely to create petty irritation as anything else. Such, for example,
has been the consequence of shopping and celebratory forays
carried out across the Sound by great numbers of Copenhageners
and Scanians.

Repeated personal contact leads to relationships not defined by
but not disruptive of the national catechism: to the extent that
friends, relatives, or business associates from a neighboring Nordic
country do not fit the prevailing stereotypes, they are considered to
be atypical; if they do fit a stereotype, this fact is used to justify the
static image. Attitudes toward national character are self-verifying.
Even if increased contact should lead to greater mutual understanding, the consequences would not necessarily be integrative.
Irrational antipathy might merely be replaced by reasoned apprehension. Finally, unless the power to make decisions becomes
centralized, even institutionalized contacts do not lead to integration: "Mutual responsiveness and unbroken links of communication among political parties, interest groups and civil servants
across national frontiers are more a result than a cause of integration." [10]

So far, new schemes for increased Scandinavian cooperation
have been hedged with guarantees that consultation would not lead
to compulsion, or have been defeated in the absence of such
guarantees. The success of measures of cooperation has made
Nordic integration even less urgent. Uniform laws, the passport
union, the growing common labor market, and social security
reciprocity all act to reduce the inconvenience of separateness. In
1966, as an implementation of Article 31 of the Helsinki Agreement, salaried consular officers were instructed to serve citizens of

[9] W. R. Mead, *An Economic Geography of the Scandinavian States and
Finland* (London: University of London Press, 1958), p. 22.
[10] Ernst B. Haas, "Persistent Themes in Atlantic and European Unity,"
World Politics, X, No. 4 (July 1958), 628.

all Scandinavian countries, whenever the person in need found no consulate of his own nationality at the location in question. Other irritations and inefficiencies will surely continue to be removed. The impact of economic collaboration within EFTA also lessens the advantage of purely Nordic efforts.

Scandinavia provides a negative example of the principle that formal integration must start with a constitutive political act. When the prospective units for union, federation, confederation, or supranationality are nation-states, the revolutionary act must be based either on coercion or on universal voluntary agreement. If the latter, then it takes unanimity to abolish the requirement of unanimity.

It follows that the number of Scandinavian states is presently fixed at five. A new unitary or federal superstate is precluded by the fact that each of the existing bodies politic wills its own continuance, and none would attempt to absorb another. That the use of force has been abandoned in inter-Scandinavian relations is recorded by Raymond E. Lindgren.[11] Nor are the tests of supranationality met in Scandinavia. There is no independent central organ which makes binding decisions by majority vote.[12] Ernst Haas defines political integration as "the process whereby political actors in several distinct national settings are persuaded to shift their loyalties, expectations and political activities toward a new center, whose institutions possess or demand jurisdiction over the pre-existing national States."[13] Regional governmental organization in the Nordic countries produces advisory opinions, weakly formu-

[11] Raymond E. Lindgren, *Norway-Sweden: Union, Disunion and Scandinavian Integration* (Princeton, N.J.: Princeton University Press, 1959). As coauthor of the work cited in footnote 5, above, Lindgren is caught in the Alice-in-Wonderland vocabulary of Karl Deutsch, wherein "integration" means "peaceful change" (*Norway-Sweden,* pp. 4–5). Thus, Scandinavia became "integrated" in 1905, when Norway seceded from union with Sweden without bloodshed, although secession is also a mark of failure to integrate (p. 6). Later, in Chapter XIV, "The Achievement of Integration," Lindgren uses the word to mean "cooperation," which, while slightly strained, at least avoids self-contradiction. Most of Lindgren's book is not marred by this terminological confusion, which the author himself notes in footnote 2, p. 4.

[12] See Ernst B. Haas, *The Uniting of Europe* (Stanford, Calif.: Stanford University Press, 1958), pp. 34–38.

[13] *Ibid.,* p. 16. See also Leon N. Lindberg, *The Political Dynamics of European Economic Integration* (Stanford, Calif.: Stanford University Press, 1963), p. 6.

lated so as to avoid dissent. Binding agreements are reached only through unanimous accord negotiated by instructed delegates and ratified by the governments. Scandinavian statesmen are without illusion on this score. The erstwhile Norwegian Foreign Minister, for example, asserts that "the Northern countries do not form a political or economic union of any sort. Nor do they constitute a bloc in the modern sense of the word. They remain five independent States, which on a regional basis try to solve problems by mutual cooperation." [14]

Cooperation, then, is the keynote of Scandinavian regionalism. It is the only alternative to isolation when integration is refused and the use of force is abandoned. "Cooperation" means peaceful change by persistent joint efforts to increase mutual advantage. Successful cooperation attempts to maximize total benefit, but there must always be mutually recognized reciprocal gain. This has been the consistent practice in Northern Europe. Occasionally, it is made explicit. In the debate on economic cooperation at the first annual session of the Nordic Council, Bertel Dahlgaard, a leading Radical Liberal and later Danish Minister for Nordic Economic Cooperation, noted that "in Denmark, we are quite agreed that in this area one cannot go farther than each country wants to go and can gladly go, and not farther than popular opinion in each single country [permits]." [15] Similarly, in the March 7, 1956, debate on foreign policy in the Swedish Parliament, Foreign Minister Östen Undén stated that Sweden was opposed to trying to persuade Norway to accept any arrangement which Norway did not herself desire or which Norway thought to be nationally disadvantageous. [16]

The Scandinavian experience demonstrates that much can be accomplished through intergovernmental cooperation. This lesson

[14] Halvard Lange, "Scandinavian Co-operation in International Affairs," *International Affairs*, XXX (1954), 285. See also his "The Northern Countries and Europe: Some Norwegian Viewpoints," *The Norseman*, VIII, No. 1 (January–February, 1950), 1–9.

[15] *1953 Record*, col. 214. Dahlgaard reiterated this view in *1955 Record*, p. 57.

[16] See Östen Undén, "Det nordiska samarbetet måste vila på den fria övertygelsens grundval" ("Nordic Cooperation Must Rest on the Foundation of Free Conviction"), *Nordisk Kontakt*, No. 4 (1956), p. 30. Undén was repeating remarks which he made at the fourth annual session of the Nordic Council; see *1956 Record*, pp. 247–48.

is particularly relevant for developing nations whose leaders do not wish to relinquish power to a higher central authority or whose people do not want to submerge their identity in a larger whole. Norwegian opposition to Nordic integration supports the observation that recency of independence is associated with exclusive nationalism. (The converse is not always the case.) The only successful examples of peaceful integration in this century have taken place since World War II among the mature and democratic nations of Western Europe. Except for Communist areas, the rest of the globe has experienced fragmentation, sometimes ameliorated by rudimentary regional cooperation. Regional cooperation short of integration in former colonial areas is seen in the recent free trade agreements entered into in Central America, Latin America, the Middle East, Southeast Asia, and West Africa.

Institutional transplantation is risky business. By virtue of formlessness, the techniques of cooperation developed by Scandinavian cabinet members and civil servants might carry over to relations among elites in neighboring emerging nations. The great advantage of these techniques is in the breadth of subjects—running the full gamut of topics of modern social legislation—to which they can be applied. The Scandinavians have erected a halfway house between the lowest-common-denominator basis of compromise which typifies traditional intergovernmental negotiations, and what Ernst Haas calls "splitting the difference" and "upgrading common interests," which are characteristic of compromise in supranational systems.[17]

The interparliamentary aspects of Nordic collaboration would seem to have relevance only for countries with representative government. The Atlantic community is nearly the only region which is so characterized. Within it, other groupings than the Scandinavian have already developed their own interparliamentary bodies, such as the Council of Europe, the Western European Union Assembly, the joint Assembly of "Little Europe" (serving EEC, ECSC, and Euratom), the Benelux Inter-Parliamentary Consultative Council, and the NATO Parliamentarians' Conferences.

[17] See Ernst B. Haas, "Technocracy, Pluralism and the New Europe," in Stephen R. Graubard (ed.), *A New Europe?* (Boston: Houghton Mifflin, 1964), pp. 65–66. This article has also been published by the Institute of International Studies, University of California, Berkeley, as General Series Reprint No. 147.

The specifics of Scandinavian regionalism may not be transferable, but the spirit is. The Nordic countries provide a case study in successful cooperation salvaged from thwarted integration. While Belgium, France, Germany, Holland, Italy, and Luxemburg are creating a new supranational entity, Denmark, Finland, Iceland, Norway, and Sweden demonstrate novel and effective techniques of accomplishing peaceful change within the nation-state system. The Nordic experience is less dramatic, but it has perhaps the broader applicability in a world which is still characterized by the predominance of nationalism. The five swans of the North fly together in remarkable harmony.

APPENDIX A: THE STATUTE

OF THE NORDIC COUNCIL,

ANNOTATED

The Statute was adopted in 1952 by the parliaments of Denmark, Iceland, Norway, and Sweden. It was amended in 1955 to provide for Finnish accession. The 1957 amendments reflect the experience of the first five years of operation. Formally, changes in the Statute are not by piecemeal amendment, but by parallel enactment in the five legislatures of a new Statute superseding the old.

The following is the author's translation of the current Statute, collated from the Danish, Norwegian, and Swedish originals, and based substantially on an unofficial mimeographed translation prepared from the Danish original by the secretariat of the Danish delegation to the Nordic Council.

Article I. The Nordic Council is an organ for consultation between the Folketing of Denmark, the Riksdag of Finland, the Althing of Iceland, the Storting of Norway and the Riksdag of Sweden, as well as the governments of these countries, in matters involving joint action by any or all of the countries.

1957 amendments: The Norwegian and Swedish versions were changed to conform to the perhaps slightly broader competence given by the Danish and Icelandic versions—the difference was subtle. The several versions are now closely parallel: linguistic experts were used to find synonymous homonyms wherever possible.

1955 amendments: Finland joined the Nordic Council, and was included in the Statute. At the same time, the word "Folketing" was substituted for "Rigsdag" to conform to internal developments in Denmark, where the 1953 Constitution provided for a new unicameral Parliament.

Article II. The Council shall consist of sixty-nine elected members and of ministerial representatives.

For such terms and by such methods as shall be decided in each country, the Folketing of Denmark, the Riksdag of Finland, the Storting of Norway and the Riksdag of Sweden shall each elect sixteen members to the Council and the requisite number of deputy delegates, and the Althing of Iceland shall elect from among its members five members to the Council and the requisite number of deputy delegates. Among the elected members of each country, different political opinions shall be represented.

Each government may appoint from among its members as many ministerial representatives as it desires.

1957 amendments: The word "member" was broadened to include ministerial representatives explicitly.

The right of Iceland to elect deputy delegates, not specified in the 1952 Statute, was formally established; this technical omission did not deter Iceland from naming alternates to the earlier sessions.

1955 amendments: These were the same as those indicated for Article I.

Article III. The ministerial representatives have no vote in the Council.

1957 amendments: Previously, the ministerial representatives were directed "not to participate in the decisions of the Council." This might have been construed to permit ministers to vote on matters not technically decisions, such as in procedural questions or in committee deliberations—although it could equally be argued that any vote is a decision. To avoid ambiguity, the precise "no vote" language was substituted. This was already the clear import of the 1952 Icelandic text.

1955 amendments: Article III originally provided for *ad hoc* participation by Finland; it was never used. With Finnish membership in the Council, the article became superfluous and was deleted. The present Article III is taken from the former last paragraph of Article II. The transfer was made to avoid renumbering all the subsequent articles. Esthetically, it might have been preferable to transfer one more paragraph from Article II, thereby keeping together the provisions for ministerial participation.

1952 contention: As originally proposed, the Statute provided that the Prime Ministers and Foreign Ministers, or their deputies, would each have a vote in the Council. At the March, 1952, meeting in Copenhagen of the Foreign Ministers of Denmark, Norway, and Sweden and the Icelandic diplomatic representative to Denmark, this provision was deleted, by unanimous agreement. Deletion was at the request of the Norwegian Foreign Minister, pursuant to resolution of the Norwegian group of the Nordic Inter-Parliamentary Union.

Article IV. The Council shall meet once a year on such date as it may decide (ordinary session). Additional sessions shall be held when the Council so decides, or when requested by at least two governments or at least twenty-five elected members (extraordinary session). Ordinary sessions shall be held in one of the capitals of the countries, as decided by the Council.

1957 amendments: The number of members required to call an extraordinary session was increased from twenty to twenty-five, in order to make allowance for the larger total membership brought about by Finland's accession. Also, by clear implication, it was provided that extraordinary sessions might be held outside the capitals or even outside Scandinavia.

Article V. For each ordinary session and for the period until the next ordinary session, the Council shall elect a President and four Vice-Presidents from among the elected members. The President and Vice-Presidents constitute the Presidium of the Council.

1957 amendments: The practice, intended by the original framers, of choosing the officers from among the elected members, was made explicit. The term of office was also clarified as running from ordinary session to ordinary session, regardless of intervening extraordinary sessions.

1955 amendments: The number of Vice-Presidents was increased to four from the previous three, to make allowance for Finnish entry into the Council.

Article VI. The deliberations of the Council shall be public, unless, in view of the special nature of a given subject, the Council decides otherwise.

This article has been construed to apply only to plenary meetings, and such was clearly the intention of the original draftsmen. All smaller gatherings, such as those of the committees or Presidium, are closed to the public. See the Directions for Committee Work, below, Appendix C, Sections 1 and 3.

Article VII. At each ordinary session the elected members shall be divided into standing committees in order to prepare matters before the Council. By decision of the Presidium, the standing committees may also meet between sessions.

Special committees may be set up to prepare special matters between sessions.

1957 amendments: It was not practicable for the Council as a whole to decide on the interim activity of standing committees, and this responsibility was delegated to the Presidium as early as the second session (*1954 Record,* p. 1015). In 1957, this provision was put in the Statute, and the practice of setting up smaller interim committees was also dignified by inclusion in the Statute.

Article VIII. The delegation of each country shall appoint a Secretary-General and other staff members. The activities and collaboration of the secretariats shall be supervised by the Presidium.

1952 contention: It was proposed that the Secretary-General from the country of the next impending ordinary session would be the chief Secretary-General. At their March, 1952, meeting, the ministers deleted such provision from Article VIII, and also removed any implication that the secretariats might undertake extensive independent research activities.

Article IX. Each government and every member is entitled to submit a matter to the Council by written application to the Presidium. The Presidium shall cause such studies to be made as it may deem necessary and shall send the pertinent documents to the governments and members well before the session.

1957 amendments: Formerly, this article provided that documents should be transmitted to the Presidium through the national secretariats; this procedure is now included in the Rules of Procedure, Section 3. The instruction to the Presidium to cause necessary studies to be made was formerly inferred from a dependent clause.

The governments are now explicitly included among those who are to receive documents before each session; this had always been the practice.

In the light of the new wording of Article II, making ministerial representatives "members" of the Council, there is some ambiguity in the word "member" as used in Article IX. In any event, no minister would introduce a matter without the prior consent of his cabinet colleagues. The restricted phrase "elected member" is used in Articles IV, V, and VII, but not in Article X.

1952 contention: At their March, 1952, meeting, the ministers acceded to the Norwegian request that the authority to initiate studies be taken from the national secretariats and given to the Presidium.

Article X. The Council shall discuss questions of common interest to the countries and may adopt recommendations to the governments. Recommendations shall be accompanied by information as to how each member has voted.

In questions which concern certain of the countries exclusively, only the members from those countries may vote.

This article is a second statement of purpose, in effect, and a broader one than that found in Article I. In practice, matters considered have been intended to result in common action and not merely in individual, albeit more enlightened, action in matters with little transnational impact.

1957 amendments: The phrase "The Council has as its purpose the discussion of . . ." was changed to the present initial phrase, "The Council shall. . . ." There is no substantive difference, but the formal existence of two different statements of purpose is avoided.

The second paragraph of Article X was narrowed to exclude non-concerned members from voting only, and not from debate, as might have been implied from the earlier wording. In practice, members from all the countries debate and vote on all matters, including those whose direct import for some of the countries is negligible or nonexistent.

The former third paragraph of this article was deleted. It provided that the Council should decide on its own organization and on the work of the secretariats. Such a provision was superfluous in the light of Article XII, directing the Council to adopt its own Rules of Procedure.

Article XI. At each ordinary session, the governments should inform the Council of the action which has been taken on the recommendations of the Council.

1952 contention: At their March, 1952, meeting the ministers softened the language of this article by adding the conditional helper verb "should."

Article XII. The Council shall adopt its own Rules of Procedure.

Article XIII. Each country shall defray the expenses of its own participation in the Council.

The Council shall decide how common expenses shall be apportioned.

1957 amendments: The article was simplified, and the statement that the host country will defray the costs of its session was transferred to

Section 21 of the Rules of Procedure. In paragraph ii, the word "defrayed" was deleted, as the Council has no means of payment of its own, and the word "apportioned" was substituted.

Former Articles XIV and XV.

These articles provided that the 1952 Statute would come into effect when adopted by Denmark, Norway, and Sweden, and, thereafter, as to Iceland when adopted by Iceland. (The next regular session of Parliament was more distant in Iceland than in other countries.) Articles XIV and XV were never included in the Icelandic version of the Statute.

1957 amendments: Articles XIV and XV were repealed, as of January 1, 1958. This date was included in each national bill or resolution, and not in the revised Statute itself.

1955 amendments: Articles XIV and XV were not amended in 1955. The 1955 amendments took effect when adopted by all the charter members and when adopted by Finland along with the Statute itself.

1952 contention: At their March, 1952, meeting, the ministers agreed to use parallel enactment instead of a treaty, as had been suggested by the Danes. Thus, a provision for renunciation of treaty by six months' notice, as found in the original draft of Article XV, became superfluous and was deleted.

APPENDIX B: THE RULES OF

PROCEDURE OF THE NORDIC

COUNCIL, ANNOTATED

After their initial adoption in 1953, the Rules of Procedure were amended at each annual session up to and including the one in 1957. Since then, only two sections of the Rules have been changed, one at the 1960 session and one at the 1962 session.

The following is the author's translation of the Rules of Procedure as last amended on March 18, 1962, collated from the Danish, Norwegian, and Swedish originals, and based preliminarily on an unofficial translation into English of the Rules as amended on February 22, 1957, prepared from the Danish by the secretariat of the Danish delegation to the Nordic Council.

Section 1. Ordinary sessions and extraordinary sessions decided upon by the Council shall begin at such time as shall have been decided by the Council in pursuance of Article IV of the Statute of the Nordic Council. The Council may, however, leave it to the Presidium to fix the time for the opening of a session. In special circumstances, the Presidium may, with the consent of all the delegations, fix a time and a place for the session which is different from that which the Council has fixed.

If at least two governments or at least twenty-five elected members desire an extraordinary session to be convened, they shall submit a written request to that effect to the Presidium. Unless the Council has decided otherwise, the extraordinary session shall be held in such place and begin at such time as the Presidium may fix, if possible in consultation with the delegations.

The Presidium shall see that the governments and elected members and their deputies are advised of the time and place for a session three months before it begins. In special circumstances, notices convening extraordinary sessions may be sent out later.

Sessions will terminate when the matters included in the agenda referred to in Section 9 have been finally decided upon or deferred to a later session.

1957 amendment: In conformity with Article IV of the Statute, as amended in 1957, twenty-five elected members, rather than twenty, are needed to call an extraordinary session. This change was occasioned by Finland's entry into the Council.

Section 2. The matters referred to in Article IX of the Statute may be brought before the Council by an elected member as a delegate's proposal, by a government as a governmental proposal, by a memorandum of the type referred to in Article XI of the Statute, or by a report on Scandinavian cooperation. Such communications shall be submitted through the country's secretariat.

A deputy delegate to the Council may, in conjunction with an elected member, introduce a delegate's proposal.

A delegate's proposal or a governmental proposal shall contain a proposal for a Council decision, except that a governmental proposal may merely contain a request for a statement of views.

1957 amendments: Provision for transmission of matters through the respective secretariat was transferred from the Statute, Article IX, to the Rules, Section 2.

The practice of allowing deputy delegates to join in introducing matters was legitimized. It had already been accepted by the national delegations, and this acceptance was noted by the Presidium at a meeting on May 3, 1954. See *1955 Record,* p. 710.

Section 3. A governmental proposal or a member's proposal must be submitted to a secretariat not later than two months before an ordinary session begins in order to be eligible for consideration by that session. In special cases the Presidium may reduce this period to one month, provided that this does not materially impair a necessary study. The memoranda and reports referred to in Section 2 shall be submitted to a secretariat not later than one month before the session begins. Governmental proposals and member's proposals, together with such studies as the Presidium may have found necessary, as well as memoranda and reports, shall be forwarded to the governments, members and deputy delegates as soon as possible and not later than three weeks before the session begins.

If the Council decides to hold an extraordinary session, a time limit shall also be fixed for raising any matter for consideration by that session. The Council may decide that only certain matters shall be considered by an extraordinary session.

Extraordinary sessions held in pursuance of Section 1, paragraph ii, shall deal only with such matters as the Council has been convened to consider. All documents shall be circulated as soon as possible.

Regardless of the provisions of this section, the Council may decide, by a majority of two-thirds, to admit a matter for consideration.

1957 amendments: In an attempt to stop wholesale dispensation, the phrase "in special cases" was added to Section 3, paragraph i, as a qualification of the power of the Presidium to reduce the time for submission of proposals from two months to one month before the opening of a session.

Section 4. In deferred matters or in matters which have been brought before the Council in accordance with Section 3 by a governmental proposal or a delegate's proposal before the beginning of a session, a government or a member may submit written proposals (amendatory proposals) up to the time when the matter is referred to committee. In connection with a memorandum or a report, proposals (supplementary proposals) may be submitted in the same way, not later than seven days before a session begins. Rules governing the possibility of submitting proposals at a later stage will be found in Section 15.

1954 amendments: Previously, amendatory and supplementary proposals could be introduced any time before the matter to which they refer was sent to committee. This was changed in 1954 to require that such proposals be made: (a) any time before referral to committee as to members' and governmental proposals, and (b) at least seven days before the session as to memoranda and reports.

Section 5. If a governmental proposal or a delegate's proposal or an amendatory or supplementary proposal is withdrawn, a member of the Council may, at the meeting at which the withdrawal is announced, adopt such proposal for consideration.

This provision has never been used. It is not clear whether the word "member" includes ministerial representatives. See the discussion of Article IX of the Statute.

Section 6. On the basis of notices to the secretariats, which should be sent in not later than one week before the beginning of each session, a list of members shall be prepared for the session. The list of members shall be approved at the first meeting of the session. Should the need arise, the list shall be amended.

The list of members will be arranged alphabetically, ministerial representatives being listed first, followed by elected members. The members will take their seats in the meeting hall in that order.

1957 amendments: A provision was deleted which required that the list of members indicate if "a member's right to participate in the Council's decisions is limited with regard to certain matters." This provision was meant to apply to Finnish members, who might be participating on an *ad hoc* basis pursuant to Article III of the Statute as it read prior to 1957. See also Section 25 of the Rules of Procedure.

Section 7. The President and Vice-Presidents shall be elected at the first meeting of each session; in these elections, provision must be made for each country and for different political opinions to be represented in the Presidium. Pending such election, the previous President shall preside over the deliberations.

Anyone who presides over or has previously presided over debate on a matter may take part in the decision, but not in the debate.

This section was not amended to conform to the 1957 amendment to Article V of the Statute, which provided that the election of the Presidium should run from ordinary session to ordinary session, irrespective of extraordinary sessions. Of course, the Statute controls.

Section 8. The Secretary of a session shall be the Secretary of the delegation in whose country the session is held. Such additional personnel as the Presidium may order shall assist in the execution of the secretarial duties.

1957 amendments: The Presidium as a whole was made responsible for securing additional personnel during a session, inasmuch as the outgoing President, who was previously the only one charged with this duty, is of a different country than that of the upcoming session.

Section 9. An agenda shall be adopted at the first meeting of a session. The agenda shall contain matters raised in pursuance of Section 3 or carried over from a previous session; the Council may, however, omit such memoranda from the agenda as do not require consideration by the session. Any matters admitted later shall likewise be included in the agenda.

1957 amendments: The Council authorized itself to omit from the agenda those memoranda which need no consideration. Such permission has not been used. Instead, matters have been considered without reference to committee, pursuant to Section 12 of the Rules of Procedure.

Section 10. At the first meeting of a session the Council shall decide what standing committees shall be set up and shall elect members to such committees. In such elections diversified representation on each standing committee shall be aimed at.

Each standing committee shall elect from among its members a Chairman and a Vice-Chairman.

1957 amendments: Previously, this section had authorized each standing committee to elect as many as three vice-chairmen, presumable so that each country (before Finnish accession) would have one officer on each committee. The practice developed, however, starting at the first session, of electing only one vice-chairman. Each country thus had one committee chairman and one committee vice-chairman. In 1957, this procedure was memorialized by inclusion in the Rules.

Section 11. Council meetings shall be held at such time as the Council or the Presidium may decide.

Giving regard to whatever the Council may have decided on the consideration of matters, the President shall prepare an agenda for each meeting; however, the outgoing Presidium shall decide the agenda for the first meeting of a session. Questions concerning the working arrangements for the current session may be raised without having been included in the agenda.

Notice of meetings shall be [posted] in the premises of the Council by 4:00 P.M. on the day before the meeting, or announced at [an earlier] meeting not later than that same day; in urgent cases notice may be given by personal communication to all delegates.

Section 12. The Council shall refer the matters included in the agenda to standing committees as soon as possible. Before a matter is referred to a standing committee, the Council members are entitled to comment on it. However, a matter may be decided without reference to committee by unanimous decision of the Council.

A matter which has been considered by a standing committee may first be taken up for decision on the second day after the committee proposal has been received by the Council. The Council may, however, decide that the matter shall be considered sooner.

A given matter shall be decided upon at the meeting for which the standing committee proposal has been placed on the agenda, unless the Council decides to postpone it to a later meeting or a later session.

Questions which relate only to the internal workings of the Council may be decided upon without reference to committee.

1957 amendments: The two-day delay on consideration of committee reports was conformed to practice by extending it to cover all reports, not just nonunanimous ones or ones which did not do as much as the author wanted, as had been the previous requirement.

Section 13. Whenever it is found necessary, a standing committee may elect a spokesman for any matter referred to it. A minority of a standing committee may also elect a spokesman.

A standing committee may invite other Council members and also cabinet members who are not representatives to the Council to take part in the committee's deliberations without, however, having any right to vote. The committee may also otherwise invite persons outside the Council to give information or make statements to it.

A member of a standing committee who is precluded by Article X, paragraph 2, of the Statute from taking part in the decision of a matter cannot take part in committee decisions either.

In the event of a tie in a standing committee, the chairman shall have the casting vote. Any member of a standing committee is entitled to submit a proposal which differs from that submitted by the committee.

Proposals from a standing committee, accompanied by reservations (minority proposals), shall be submitted to the Council in writing.

Section 14. In the course of the Council's deliberations, members will be permitted to speak in the order in which they have asked for the floor. The presiding officer may deviate from this order, subject to the approval of the Council.

On the presiding officer's proposal, the Council may restrict speakers to limited periods in a debate. On the presiding officer's proposal, or on the proposal of five of the Council's elected members, the Council may decide, by a majority of two-thirds, to close debate on a matter.

The proposals referred to in paragraph ii cannot be debated.

In the Swedish version, paragraph iii is simply the final sentence of paragraph ii, and reads as follows: "No debate can take place on such proposals."

Section 15. A recommendation on any matter included in the agenda may be adopted if it is within the framework of a governmental proposal, a member's proposal, an amendatory proposal or a supplementary proposal, or if it is otherwise in conformity with proposals which the Council has consented to admit for consideration. Such consent is also required when, in the course of Council debate, a member presents a proposal for a recommendation which is not occasioned by the report of a standing committee.

Decisions on recommendations shall be taken by roll call according to the list of members. The answer to a roll call may be either "Yes" or "No" or "Abstain." A recommendation is adopted when more than half of those members present who are entitled to vote in the matter have voted yes.

If several incompatible proposals for a recommendation on a matter have been submitted, the presiding officer shall decide the sequence in which votes shall be taken. The presiding officer shall announce this sequence to the Council before the debate, if possible, and at the latest before the voting begins.

1962 amendment: The last sentence of paragraph ii of Section 15 was changed to require a qualified majority of those eligible to vote (pursuant to Article X of the Statute). Previously, the sentence in question required only a simple majority, as follows: "A recommendation is adopted when more have voted for the proposal than against it."

1957 amendments: A new paragraph was added, giving the presiding officer discretion in determining the sequence in which votes shall be taken.

1955 amendments: The requirement was added that all new proposals made during a session must be within the framework of an original proposal in the absence of Council consent to the contrary.

Section 16. In elections, voting shall be by secret ballot if one member so desires. In the event of a tie, lots shall be drawn. The working committees of the delegations, referred to in Section 25, shall submit nominations for elections held in pursuance of Sections 7 and 10, paragraph i.

Section 17. In cases other than those referred to in Sections 15 or 16, decisions shall be taken by open vote if more than one proposal has been submitted or if one elected member so desires. If for special reasons the Presidium finds that a decision is not required, the presiding officer may omit the taking of a vote on the question under consideration.

An open vote is taken by the members rising from their seats. The vote shall show how many of the delegates present have voted either "Yes" or "No" or have abstained. In the event of a tie, the presiding officer has the casting vote. If more than one vote is required, then the provisions of Section 15, paragraph iii, shall apply.

If one elected member so desires, a vote shall be taken by roll call according to the rules of Section 15, paragraph ii, instead of by open vote.

1957 and 1955 amendments: The voting procedures were spelled out in more detail.

Section 18. The Council and standing committees form a quorum when at least one-half of their elected members are present. If, under Article X, paragraph 2, of the Statute, only members from certain countries may take part in the consideration of a matter, the Council and the standing committees form a quorum when at least one-half of the elected members from those countries are present.

There is no quorum provision for special committees. Special committees meet between sessions (Statute, Article VII, paragraph 2) and may include nonmembers of the Council (Rules, Section 23). Special committees were first mentioned in the Statute of the Nordic Council in 1957 (Article VII, paragraph 2), and Section 18 of the Rules of Procedure has not since been expanded to include them.

Section 19. The Secretary shall arrange for minutes to be kept of Council meetings, containing a shorthand report of the deliberations. The minutes shall be approved by the Presidium.

The Secretary shall arrange for the minutes to be printed, except for those parts which deal with meetings which are closed to the public.

Section 20. Recommendations shall be signed by the President and countersigned by the Secretary. The result of votes taken on proposals for recommendations shall be communicated to the governments, whether such proposals have been adopted or rejected.

Section 21. The cost of printing and other common expenses referred to in Article XIII of the Statute shall be apportioned among the countries in proportion to the number of elected members to the Council. Each country shall, however, defray the special cost of meetings held in that country. In special cases, the Presidium can fix a different apportionment.

1960 amendment: The last sentence was added. In some cases, Nordic Council reports do not affect all the member nations; the new provision permits the cost of such reports to be divided among the countries concerned only. This problem had arisen in 1958, in that the massive reports on the proposed common Nordic market did not relate to Iceland. On this occasion the Council voted to accept the Presidium's proposal that the printing costs be divided equally between Denmark, Finland, Norway, and Sweden. *1958 Record,* pp. 224, 1598, 1912.

1957 amendments: This provision was transferred to the Rules of Procedure from Article XIII of the Statute.

Section 22. During the periods between sessions the Presidium shall be responsible for the conduct of the Council's current activities. The Presidium shall report to each ordinary session on its activities since the last ordinary session.

The Presidium shall provide for the management of the activities of the secretariats and for their mutual cooperation, for which the Presidium is responsible under Article VIII of the Statute. The direct management of the secretariat of each country shall be undertaken by that country's representative on the Presidium.

The Presidium may take unanimous decisions without holding a meeting.

1957 amendments: Provision was made for an annual report on interim activities, conforming to earlier practice.

1954 amendments: The interim duties of the Presidium were specified.

Section 23. Persons other than members and deputy delegates can only be appointed members of a special committee in exceptional cases. A special committee shall report on its activities at ordinary sessions.

1957 amendments: This section was added in its entirety to give recognition to the existence of the special committees. (See the discussion of Article VII of the Statute.) It was amended in committee (*1957 Record,* pp. 1526–31) to emphasize that special committee members will ordinarily be Elected Members or Deputy Delegates to the Council.

Section 24 [formerly Section 23]. If a member of the Presidium or of a standing committee becomes temporarily or permanently unable to take part in the work between sessions or ceases to be a member of the Council, he shall be replaced by a member appointed by the delegation to which he belongs.

Between sessions, a member of a special committee or his alternate shall be appointed by the delegation of his country.

1957 amendments: This section was renumbered, and paragraph ii was added to it.

Section 25 [formerly Section 24]. Each delegation shall elect a working committee to consult with the Presidium and with the other working committees on questions concerning the organization of the Council's activities.

1957 amendments: This section was renumbered.

1956 amendments: The original Section 25 was deleted. It had provided for *ad hoc* Finnish participation in Council activities, but was never used. Between February 1, 1956, and February 22, 1957, when the present Section 25 was adopted, there was no Section 25.

Section 26. In special cases, the Council may decide by a two-thirds majority to depart from the provisions of these Rules of Procedure.

The Rules of Procedure are adopted and amended by majority vote. Thus, they are more easily amended than suspended. Furthermore, either amendment or suspension would be easier to effect than the occasional requirement of unanimity (e.g., Section 12 of the Rules, providing for exemption from the requirement of referral to committee). Moreover, the specific requirement of a two-thirds vote for waiver of particular provisions (e.g., Section 3 of the Rules, permitting matters to be admitted for Council decision which do not meet the conditions enumerated elsewhere in Section 3) would seem superfluous in the light of the availability of Section 26.

APPENDIX C: THE DIRECTIONS

FOR COMMITTEE WORK,

ANNOTATED

The Directions for Committee Work are extraconstitutional. No authorization for them is found in the Statute or Rules of Procedure of the Nordic Council. In 1953, the Directions took the form of suggestions emerging from a conference between the Presidium and the committee chairmen. Thereafter, the formulation of the Directions was taken over by the Joint Working Committee, and the tone became one of command.

The following is the author's translation of the 1964 Swedish version. It has been collated, where feasible, with the earlier Swedish versions (1955 and 1957 through 1963) and with the 1956 Danish version and the 1954 Norwegian version.

Paragraph 1. The first meeting of the committee shall be brought to order by the member whose name stands first on the alphabetically prepared list of members elected to the committee.

At this meeting:

a. a chairman and vice-chairman shall be elected;

b. it shall be announced who has been appointed secretary to the committee by the Presidium, pursuant to Section 8 of the Rules of Procedure of the Council;

c. those members of the Council who are ministerial representatives shall be invited to participate in committee deliberations, unless specifically decided otherwise;

d. the committee shall authorize the chairman in every particular case to permit elected members as well as deputy delegates to the Council to attend committee deliberations;

e. the committee shall decide which experts should be summoned to the committee pursuant to Section 13, paragraph ii, of the Rules of Procedure of the Council, in order to assist the committee with regard to the various matters (the Presidium having established a list of persons who, in its opinion, can be considered as such experts);

f. the committee shall establish a preliminary program for its work.

For convenience, each section of Paragraph 1 will be annotated separately, as follows:

"Paragraph 1. The first meeting of the committee shall be brought to order by the member whose name stands first on the alphabetically prepared list of members elected to the committee."

This sentence was first included in the Directions in 1955. No essential changes have been made in it since then.

"At this meeting:
"a. a chairman and vice-chairman shall be elected; . . ."

This section was added in 1954. It contained a provision for election of the secretary which, in 1955, became section b. Otherwise, no essential changes have been made.

["At this meeting:]
"b. it shall be announced who has been appointed secretary to the committee by the Presidium, pursuant to Section 8 of the Rules of Procedure of the Council; . . ."

This section was transferred from the preceding section in 1955, at which time it was corrected to become a mere announcement of presidential selection, rather than a direction for committee election. It was changed in 1957 to conform to the 1957 amendment to Section 8 of the Rules of Procedure, which directed that the Presidium as a whole should engage personnel for sessions, rather than the President alone.

["At this meeting:]
"c. those members of the Council who are ministerial representatives shall be invited to participate in committee deliberations, unless specifically decided otherwise; . . ."

Since 1954 this section has remained essentially the same as the current version. In 1953, it read as follows:

"Paragraph 6. Attention is directed to the Presidium's suggestion that the *ministerial representatives* concerned *be invited* to committee meetings" (emphasis in original).

["At this meeting:]
"d. the committee shall authorize the chairman in every particular case to permit elected members as well as deputy delegates to the Council to attend committee deliberations; . . ."

In 1961, attendance by elected members from other committees was provided for; otherwise, no significant changes have been made in this section since it was first added in 1955.

["At this meeting:]
"e. the committee shall decide which experts should be summoned to the committee pursuant to Section 13, paragraph ii, of the Rules of Procedure of the Council, in order to assist the committee with regard to the various matters (the Presidium having established a list of persons who, in its opinion, can be considered as such experts); . . ."
The parenthetical material was added in 1959. Otherwise, this section has not been materially changed since it was first added in 1954.

["At this meeting:]
"f. the committee shall establish a preliminary program for its work."
Since 1954, this section has remained essentially the same as the current version. In 1953, it read as follows:
"Paragraph 7. It is suggested that on Monday, the 16th, the committee prepare a schedule for *committee work,* with the most expedient grouping of subjects" (emphasis in original).

Paragraph 2. Deliberations of the committee are closed, and the committee should not make its meetings public.

This paragraph was added in 1959. At this time, the old Paragraph 2 became Paragraph 4, and the old Paragraph 4 and all subsequent paragraphs were renumbered, each digit being increased by one.

Paragraph 3. Besides the appropriate committee secretary and those who are entitled to be present from time to time as decided upon in accordance with Paragraph 1, the members of the Presidium, the Secretaries-General to the delegations, and those who the committee has otherwise decided to summon pursuant to Section 13 of the Rules of Procedure have access to committee deliberations. The members of the Presidium and the Secretaries-General have the right to take the floor in committee, as does the committee secretary.

This provision was added in 1954. The word "summon" in the first sentence of Paragraph 3 is inappropriate, inasmuch as the corresponding word in Section 13 of the Rules of Procedure is "invite."
Section 13, paragraph ii, of the Rules of Procedure authorizes the committee to invite the following persons to attend its meetings: (1) Scandinavian cabinet members who have not been appointed to the Nordic Council as ministerial representatives, and (2) elected members

to the Nordic Council who are assigned to other committees. (Ministerial representatives to the Nordic Council are invited to committee hearings pursuant to Directions, Paragraph 1 c.)

The 1958 and 1957 versions of the first sentence of Paragraph 3 of the Directions made no provision for such invitation. They purported to define the exclusive basis for committee attendance, and were thus in conflict with the Rules of Procedure. This discrepancy was eliminated in 1959, when Section 13 authorization was incorporated into Paragraph 3 by reference.

The 1958 and 1957 versions of Paragraph 3 read as follows:

"Paragraph 3. The members of the Presidium and the Secretaries-General to the delegations have the right to attend committee deliberations and to express themselves therein, as does the committee secretary. Otherwise, persons other than those the committee has decided to summon or invite to attend the deliberations in accordance with Paragraph 1 should not be present at committee meetings.

"Observers from the young people's political organizations thus have the right to be present . . . only to the extent that they are used as experts in those questions which particularly concern youth."

It was the persistent efforts of the youth clubs to gain access to committee hearings which led to the successive amplification of the closed-committee principle, seen also in Paragraphs 1 e and 2.

The 1956, 1955, and 1954 versions of Paragraph 3, on the other hand, were short and positive, as follows:

"Paragraph 3. Members of the Presidium and the Secretaries-General have the right to attend deliberations in committee and to take the floor there, just as the committee secretary may also take the floor."

The 1959 and 1960 versions of Paragraph 3 contained an additional sentence, as follows:

"It is up to the committee itself to take a position on the presence of the experts in committee at the moment when decisions are reached."

Paragraph 4. The minutes of the committee's meetings shall be kept by the secretary, who will indicate the time of opening and closing of each meeting, the names of the members and ministerial representatives present as well as of the summoned experts, and the decisions reached by the committee.

The 1958 and 1957 versions of this paragraph were essentially the same as the current version.

The 1956 and 1955 versions were also the same, except that there was no provision for recording the names of the experts who were present; such a record was kept anyway.

The 1954 and 1953 versions were the same as the 1956 and 1955 versions, but with the addition of a single sentence, as follows:

"However, no record of the discussions shall be kept."

Paragraph 5. Each matter shall be laid before the committee by a committee member, the committee secretary, or a summoned expert. The committee is to make proposals to the Council concerning each matter referred to the committee.

Earlier versions were essentially the same as the current one, with the following exceptions:
1. the 1957 version asked the committee only for a report, and not specifically for a proposal;
2. in the 1956, 1955, and 1954 versions, there was one additional sentence, as follows:
"The secretary has the duty of formulating the report."
3. the 1953 version of Paragraph 5 read as follows:
"Paragraph 2. The committees shall decide themselves whether they will have a parliamentary secretary in addition to the appointed secretary. It is the duty of the appointed secretary to prepare the committee's report, and, when necessary, to provide materials, to the extent that this is not done by the chairman or commissioned expert."
A parliamentary secretary was chosen by each committee from among its members at the first session, but not thereafter.

Paragraph 6. A spokesman shall be appointed for each proposal to present the matter to the Council, to the extent that seems called for. In questions of greater import, the committee should prepare for debate in the Council, for example by preparing a proposal for a preliminary list of speakers for the plenary meeting.

From 1955 to 1958, this paragraph was essentially the same as the current version.
In 1954, this paragraph consisted of a single sentence, the present first sentence.
The 1953 version read as follows:
"Paragraph 3. It is recommended that each committee choose a reporter (spokesman) for each matter, with the duty of being the first speaker in the matter concerned."

Paragraph 7. The committee proposal shall contain information as to who has participated in or been present at the consideration of a matter in committee, reference to documents and other papers which have been before the committee, the basis for the decision of the committee, the decision itself, and any reservations (minority proposals). The proposal shall be formulated in the language of the person who has drafted it.

Earlier versions were essentially the same as the current version, except that the 1953 version read as follows:
"Paragraph 4. The committees ought to strive to draw up in writing in the report not only the recommendations of the committees, but also their motivation."

Paragraph 8. A form has been prepared for the drafting of decisions which should be followed, where possible, in the interests of uniformity. Where delegate's proposals and governmental proposals are concerned, and in matters in which a supplementary proposal has been made, the decision ought to point toward one of the following three alternatives: the adoption of a recommendation, a rejection (take no action), or postponement. It is presumed that reports and memoranda will be accepted, the memoranda together with an indication of whether the recommendation is considered as terminated, or whether a new memorandum is awaited at a later session.

"Reports" refers to accounts given by the permanent organs of cooperation, pursuant to Section 2 of the Rules of Procedure of the Council. "Memoranda" refers to the accounts of progress given by the governments on previous Council recommendations, pursuant to Section 2 of the Rules of Procedure and Article XI of the Statute.
The 1958 version of Paragraph 8 read as follows:
"Paragraph 7. Concerning each question which does not lead to a proposal for a recommendation or a proposal that the Council take no action in connection with the delegate's proposal, etc., the decision shall indicate if the committee considers it terminated, that its further consideration should be postponed, that it should give rise to a new memorandum, etc."
The versions from 1954 to 1957 were essentially the same as the 1958 version.
There was no corresponding paragraph in the 1953 version.

Paragraph 9. Inasmuch as the Presidium has decided that committees shall be required to meet between sessions, the chairman will have to summon his committee, thereby setting a time and place for meeting.

This paragraph was added in 1964.

APPENDIX D: TREATY OF

COOPERATION BETWEEN

DENMARK, FINLAND, ICELAND,

NORWAY, AND SWEDEN

This treaty was signed in Helsinki on March 23, 1962, and is referred to as the Helsinki Agreement. It entered into force on July 1, 1962. For the most part, the following is a translation of the treaty into English as published jointly by the Royal Swedish Ministry for Foreign Affairs and the Nordic Council.

The Governments of Denmark, Finland, Iceland, Norway and Sweden,

Desirous of furthering the close connections between the Nordic nations in culture and in juridical and social conceptions and of developing cooperation between the Nordic countries;

Endeavoring to create uniform rules in the Nordic countries in as many respects as possible;

Hoping to achieve in all fields where prerequisites exist an appropriate division of labor between these countries;

Desirous of continuing the cooperation, important to these countries, in the Nordic Council and other agencies of cooperation;

Have agreed upon the following provisions.

INTRODUCTORY PROVISION

Article 1. The contracting parties shall endeavor to maintain and further develop cooperation between the countries in the juridical, cultural, social and economic fields and in question of communications.

JURIDICAL COOPERATION

Article 2. The contracting parties shall continue the work to attain the highest possible degree of juridical equality between a national of any Nordic country, resident in a Nordic country other than his own, and the citizens of his country of residence.

Article 3. The contracting parties shall endeavor to facilitate the acquisition of citizenship by nationals of one Nordic country in another Nordic country.

Article 4. The contracting parties shall continue legislative cooperation in order to attain the greatest possible uniformity in private law.

Article 5. The contracting parties should strive to create uniform provisions regarding crime and the consequences of crime.

The investigation and prosecution of a crime committed in one Nordic country should, to the greatest possible extent, be pursued also in another Nordic country.

Article 6. The contracting parties shall strive to achieve mutual coordination of other legislation than that defined above in any fields where this proves to be appropriate.

Article 7. Each contracting party should work for the creation of such rules that a sentence passed by a court or other authority in another Nordic country can be executed also within the territory of the party in question.

CULTURAL COOPERATION

Article 8. In every Nordic country, education and training given at school shall include, in a suitable degree, instruction in the language, culture and general social conditions of the other Nordic countries.

Article 9. Each contracting party should maintain and extend the opportunities for a student from another Nordic country to pursue studies and graduate in its educational esatblishments. It should also be possible, to the greatest possible extent, to count a preliminary examination passed in any Nordic country towards a final examination taken in another Nordic country.

It should be possible to receive economic assistance from the country of domicile, irrespective of the country where the studies are pursued.

Article 10. The contracting parties should coordinate public education qualifying for a given profession or trade.

Such education should, as far as possible, have the same qualifying value in all the Nordic countries. Additional studies necessary for reasons connected with national conditions can, however, be required.

Article 11. In the fields where cooperation is expedient, the development of educational establishments should be made uniform through continuous cooperation over development plans and their implementation.

Article 12. Cooperation in the field of research should be so organized that research funds and other resources available will be coordinated and exploited in the best possible way, among other things by establishing joint institutions.

Article 13. In order to support and strengthen cultural development the contracting parties shall promote free Nordic popular education and exchange in the fields of literature, art, music, theater, film and other fields of culture; among other things, the possibilities provided by radio and television should be borne in mind.

SOCIAL COOPERATION

Article 14. The contracting parties shall strive to preserve and further develop the common Nordic labor market along the lines drawn up in earlier agreements. Labor exchanges and vocational guidance shall be coordinated. The exchange of trainees shall be free.

Efforts should be made to achieve uniformity in national regulations on industrial safety and other questions of a similar nature.

Article 15. The contracting parties shall strive for arrangements whereby it will be possible for the nationals of one Nordic country, while staying in another Nordic country, to receive, as far as possible, the same social benefits as are offered to the citizens of the country of residence.

Article 16. The contracting parties shall further develop cooperation in public health and medical care, temperance work, child welfare and youth welfare.

Article 17. Each one of the contracting parties shall strive to have medical, technical or other similar safety controls carried out in such a way that the examination certificate issued will be acceptable in the other Nordic countries.

ECONOMIC COOPERATION

Article 18. The contracting parties shall, in order to promote economic cooperation in different fields, consult one another on questions of economic policy. Attention shall be devoted to the possibilities of coordinating measures taken to level out cyclical fluctuations.

Article 19. The contracting parties intend in so far as possible, to promote cooperation between their countries in production and investment, striving to create conditions for direct cooperation between enterprises in two or more Nordic countries. In the further development of international cooperation, the contracting parties should strive to achieve an appropriate division of labor between the countries in the fields of production and investment.

Article 20. The contracting parties shall work for the greatest possible freedom of capital movement between the Nordic countries. In other payments and currency questions of common interest, joint solutions shall be sought.

Article 21. The contracting parties shall seek to consolidate the cooperation started earlier to remove barriers to trade between the Nordic countries and, to the greatest extent possible, to strengthen and develop further this cooperation.

Article 22. In issues of international commercial policy the contracting parties shall endeavor, both separately and jointly, to promote the interests of the Nordic countries and, with this purpose in view, to consult one another.

Article 23. The contracting parties shall strive for coordination of technical and administrative customs regulations and for simplification of customs procedure in order to facilitate communications between the countries.

Article 24. The regulations governing frontier trade between the Nordic countries shall be formulated in such a way as to cause a minimum of inconvenience to the inhabitants of frontier districts.

Article 25. When the need and the necessary conditions exist for joint economic development of adjoining parts of the territories of two or more contracting parties, these parties shall jointly endeavor to promote such development.

COOPERATION IN THE FIELD OF COMMUNICATIONS

Article 26. The contracting parties shall seek to consolidate the earlier cooperation in the field of traffic and seek to develop this cooperation in order to facilitate communications and the exchange of commodities between the countries and in order to find an expedient solution to problems that may arise in this field.

Article 27. The construction of traffic arteries involving the territories of two or more contracting parties shall be achieved through joint consultations between the parties concerned.

Article 28. The contracting parties shall seek to preserve and to further develop the cooperation that has resulted in making their territories into one region as regards passport inspection. The inspection of passengers crossing the frontiers between the Nordic countries shall be simplified and coordinated in other respects as well.

Article 29. The contracting parties shall coordinate the work to improve traffic safety.

OTHER COOPERATION

Article 30. The contracting parties should, whenever possible and appropriate, consult one another regarding questions of mutual interest that are dealt with by international organizations and at international conferences.

Article 31. An official in the foreign service of a contracting party who is on assignment outside the Nordic countries, shall, to the extent compatible with his official duties and if nothing gainsays it in the country to which he is appointed, also assist nationals of another Nordic country, in the event that this country has no representation in the locality concerned.

Article 32. The contracting parties should, whenever it is found possible and expedient, coordinate their activities for aid to and cooperation with the developing countries.

Article 33. Steps should be taken to spread increased knowledge of the Nordic countries and Nordic cooperation through close collaboration between the contracting parties and their agencies for foreign information service. Whenever found expedient, joint actions may be taken.

Article 34. The contracting parties shall work for the coordination of different branches of official statistics.

THE FORMS OF NORDIC COOPERATION

Article 35. In order to achieve the aims mentioned in this treaty the contracting parties should continuously consult one another and, whenever necessary, take coordinating measures.

This cooperation shall, as hitherto, take place at ministerial meetings, within the Nordic Council and its agencies in conformity with the guiding principles formulated in the Charter of the Council, through special organs of cooperation or between the authorities concerned.

Article 36. The Nordic Council should be given an opportunity to express its views on questions of Nordic cooperation that are of importance in principle, whenever this is not impossible due to lack of time.

Article 37. Regulations which have come about as a result of cooperation between two or more of the contracting parties may not be altered by one party without the other party or parties being informed thereof. However, such notice shall not be required in matters of urgency or when rules of minor importance are involved.

Article 38. The authorities in the Nordic countries may engage in direct correspondence with each other on all issues except those which by their nature or for some other reason must be dealt with through Foreign Service channels.

FINAL PROVISIONS

Article 39. This treaty shall be ratified and the instruments of ratification deposited with the Finnish Ministry for Foreign Affairs as soon as possible.

The treaty shall enter into force on the first day of the month following the date of the deposit of the ratification instruments of all the contracting parties.

Article 40. Should any of the contracting parties wish to terminate the validity of the treaty, a written notice to this effect shall be delivered to the government of Finland, which without delay shall inform the other contracting parties of the matter and of the date when the notice was received.

The termination applies only to the country which gave notice and shall become valid on the first day of the month which is six months after the date on which the government of Finland received the notice of termination.

The treaty shall be deposited with the Finnish Ministry for Foreign Affairs, and the Finnish Ministry for Foreign Affairs shall supply all contracting parties with certified copies thereof.

In witness whereof, the undersigned plenipotentiaries, duly empowered, have appended their signatures to this treaty.

Done at Helsinki, in a single copy, in the Danish, Finnish, Icelandic, Norwegian and Swedish languages, each text being equally authentic, this twenty-third day of March, nineteen hundred and sixty-two.

APPENDIX E: THE STATUTE

OF THE NORDIC

INTER-PARLIAMENTARY UNION

The following is the author's translation of the Swedish version of the Statute, as found in *Det 27. nordiska interparlamentariska delegerademötet, 1949* (Helsinki: Finlands interparlamentariska grupp, 1950), pp. 3–5.

I. Purpose—Composition

1. The Nordic Inter-Parliamentary Union is composed of the Danish, Finnish, Icelandic, Norwegian, and Swedish groups of the Inter-Parliamentary Union.

The Union's purpose, through cooperation among the groups, is to further the Union's general purposes and to consider questions of international law and other questions which are of particular interest for the Nordic countries' relations among themselves or with others—all in order to develop good mutual understanding among the Nordic peoples.

The Union's organs are the President, the Executive Board, the meeting of delegates, and the conference.

Only the Danish, Norwegian, and Swedish languages are to be used in the Union's affairs.

II. The President

2. The Chairman, or, in his absence, the Vice-Chairman, of the Inter-Parliamentary group in the country where meetings are to be held during the year shall function as President of the Union.

His term of office begins on January first.

III. The Executive Board

3. The business of the Union shall be managed by an Executive Board, consisting of the Chairman, Vice-Chairman, and two specially elected members of each group.

In addition, each group elects four alternates.

4. The President of the Union chairs the Executive Board. The Board meets at least once a year and, in addition, as often as the President finds it necessary or when at least four members of the Executive Board request it.

5. In particular, the Executive Board is directed to:
   a. prepare and call meetings of delegates and conferences;
   b. carry out decisions taken;
   c. make decisions concerning the shared expenses of the Union and their apportionment among the groups.

The Executive Board makes its own rules of procedure.

IV. Meetings of Delegates

6. Meetings of delegates are composed of the members of the Executive Board plus at most fifteen specially elected representatives from each group.

Meetings of delegates take place once a year as a rule, unless decided otherwise, in turn in each of the countries where groups adhering to the Union are found.

7. The call, which shall be issued at least a month in advance, shall as far as possible be accompanied by an indication of the items which are to be considered.

Proposals for subjects to be deliberated at meetings of delegates must reach the President by the time he specifies if they are to be taken into consideration in the preparation of the list of topics.

Deliberations will embrace those questions which the Executive Board has put on the list of topics or otherwise proposed for consideration. Other proposals and petitions will be taken up for consideration only if the meeting makes a decision to that effect after having gotten the opinion of the Executive Board and after having weighed a short explanation from the delegate who wishes the matter to be considered.

Decisions of the meetings of delegates are determinative of all the Union's affairs, except in those cases where the Statute determines otherwise.

8. The President of the Union leads the deliberations of the

meetings of delegates. The other chairmen of groups are the meetings' Vice-Presidents, and participate together with the President in the determination of questions concerning the agenda of the meetings.

The official record of a meeting and its proceedings is published and signed by the President and Vice-Presidents.

9. The Prime Ministers and Foreign Ministers of the countries where groups belonging to the Union are found ought to participate in the deliberations of the meetings of delegates.

V. The Conference

10. The Executive Board, after reaching agreement with the group in the country where the meeting is to be held during the year, may call a conference.

The right to participate in the conference belongs to all the members of the groups which adhere to the Union.

11. The provisions which are made above for meetings of delegates in Paragraphs 7, 8, and 9, apply to conferences, except that the Executive Board definitively prepares the list of topics for the conference.

VI. Amendments to the Statute

12. Proposals for amendment to this Statute can be offered by the Executive Board or by each of the groups which adhere to the Union. A proposal is adopted when it is accepted by all of the groups in unchanged form, after being first presented to a meeting of delegates or a conference.

SELECTED BIBLIOGRAPHY

SECONDARY SOURCE MATERIALS ON THE NORDIC COUNCIL
IN MAJOR WEST EUROPEAN LANGUAGES

By Members of the Presidium of the Nordic Council
or Secretaries-General to National Nordic Council Delegations

Eriksen, Erik. "The Nordic Council's Fourth Session," *Inter-Parliamentary Bulletin*, XXXVI, No. 2 (1956), 56–63.

Hedtoft, Hans. "The Nordic Council," *American-Scandinavian Review*, XLII, No. 1 (Spring, 1954), 13–21.

Herlitz, Nils. "The Nordic Council," in Jørgen Bukdahl *et al.* (ed.), *Scandinavia Past and Present* (Odense: Arnkrone, 1959), III, 43–48.

———. *Der Nordische Rat: Voraussetzungen, Aufbau, Aufgaben.* Bonn: Schriftenreihe des deutschen Rates der Europäischen Bewegung, 1955. Pp. 16.

Hønsvald, Nils. "The Second Session of the Nordic Council," *Inter-Parliamentary Bulletin*, XXXIV (November–December, 1954), 166–77.

Løchen, Einar. "A Comparative Study of Certain European Parliamentary Assemblies," *Annuaire Européen/European Yearbook* (The Hague: Nijhoff, 1958), IV, 150–73.

———. "The Nordic Council," in Kenneth Lindsay (ed.), *European Assemblies 1948–59* (London: Stevens, 1960), pp. 252–59.

Meinander, Ragnar, and Sven-Olof Hultin. "Fifth Session of the Nordic Council and the Recommendation Concerning Nuclear Energy," *Inter-Parliamentary Bulletin*, XXXVII, No. 1 (1957), 20–26.

Petrén, Gustaf. "The Nordic Council: A Unique Factor in International Law," *Nordisk Tidsskrift for International Ret*, XXIX, No. 4 (1959), 346–62.

———. "Der Nordische Rat," *Schriftenreihe zur europäischen Integration*, I (1960), 151–65.

Wendt, Frantz. *The Nordic Council and Co-operation in Scandinavia.* Copenhagen: Munksgaard, 1959. Pp. 247.

————. "The Northern Council: Its Background, Structure and First Session," *Travaux de l'Institut International de Finances Publique,* IX (1953), 199–210.

By Others

In English

Anderson, Stanley V. "Negotiations for the Nordic Council," *Nordisk Tidsskrift for International Ret,* XXXIII, No. 1–2 (1963), 23–33.

————. "The Nordic Council and the 1962 Helsinki Agreement," *Nordisk Tidsskrift for International Ret,* XXXIV, No. 4 (1964), 278–300.

Dolan, Paul. "The Nordic Council," *Western Political Quarterly,* XII, No. 2 (1959), 511–26.

Nagel, Heinrich. "The Nordic Council: Its Organs, Functions and Juridical Nature," *Annuaire Revue de l'A.A.A./Annual Journal of the A.A.A.,* XXVI (1956), 51–67.

In French

"Le Conseil Nordique et la Collaboration Scandinave," *Chronique de Politique Étrangère,* VII, No. 3 (May, 1954), 332—38.

"Le Conseil Nordique et la Coopération Scandinave," Série Internationale No. 374, *La Documentation Française: Notes et Études Documentaires,* No. 2,476 (Oct. 25, 1958), pp. 1–27.

Sorensen [Sørensen], Max. "Le Conseil Nordique," *Revue Générale de Droit International Public,* LIX, No. 1 (January–March, 1955), 63–84.

In German

Haintz, Otto. "Der Nordische Rat," *Archiv des Völkerrechts,* IV, No. 4 (October, 1954), 450–56, 472–74.

Nagel, Heinrich. "Einige rechtsvergleichende Bemerkungen zu den Empfehlungen der Vereinten Nationen, des Europarates und des Nordischen Rates," *Internationales Recht und Diplomatie,* No. 3 (1958), pp. 223–35.

————. "Lassen die Empfehlungen der Vereinten Nationen Rückschlüsse auf die rechtliche Natur der Empfehlungen des Europarates und des Nordischen Rates zu?" *Nordisk Tidsskrift for InternationalRet,* XXX, No. 1–2 (1960), 52–72.

————. "Der Nordische Rat, seine Organe, seine Funktionen, und seine Juristische Natur," *Jahrbuch für Internationales Recht,* VI (1955), 199–214.

Simson, Gerhard. "Der Nordische Rat," *Zeitschrift für Ausländisches Öffentliches Recht und Völkerrecht*, XV, No. 1–2 (October, 1953), 128–33.

SECONDARY SOURCE MATERIALS ON NORDIC COOPERATION IN MAJOR WEST EUROPEAN LANGUAGES

Andrén, Nils. "The Nordic Cultural Commission 1947–57," *The Norseman*, XV, No. 6 (November–December, 1957), 375–82.

Bellquist, Eric C. "Inter-Scandinavian Cooperation," *Annals of the American Academy of Political and Social Science*, CLXVIII (July, 1933), 183–96.

————, and Wendell C. Schaeffer. "Inter-Scandinavian Economic Co-operation," *Foreign Policy Reports*, XXIV, No. 5 (May 5, 1948), 63–64.

Boyens, John. "Integrationsprobleme für Schweden und Finnland," *Aussenpolitik*, XIV, No. 6 (June, 1963), 401–10.

————. "Die nordische Zusammenarbeit," *Europa-Archiv*, XVIII, No. 22 (1963), 845–52.

Burbank, Lyman B. "Scandinavian Integration and Western Defense," *Foreign Affairs*, XXXV, No. 1 (October, 1956), 144–50.

Dahl, Paul. "Scandinavian Integration," *Yale Review*, XLV, No. 4 (June, 1956), 634–36.

de Sydow, Gunnar. "The Scandinavian Co-operation in the Field of Legislation after the Second World War," *Unification du Droit/Unification of Law* (Rome: Unidroit, 1954), III, 486–95, in French and English.

Etzioni, Amitai. "A Stable Union: The Nordic Associational Web," in *Political Unification* (New York: Holt, Rinehart and Winston, 1965) pp. 184–228.

Eyben, W. E. von. "Inter-Nordic Legislative Co-operation," in Folke Schmidt (ed.), *Scandinavian Studies in Law* (Stockholm: Almqvist and Wiksell, 1962), VI, 63–93.

Fagerholm, K.-A. "Finland in the Nordic Family Circle," in *Introduction to Finland 1960* (Helsinki: Söderström, 1960), pp. 69–78.

Franzen, Gosta [Gösta]. "Will There Be a United States of Scandinavia?" *World Affairs Interpreter*, XV, No. 2 (July, 1944), 147–58.

Gran, Bjarne. "Norway and Northern Cooperation," *The Norseman*, XII, No. 4 (July–August, 1954), 230–33.

Herlitz, Nils. "Nordischer Gedanke und Nordische Gemeinschaft," *Aussenpolitik*, VII, No. 10 (October, 1956), 628–39.

Holly, Norman E. "Legal and Legislative Co-operation in the Scandinavian States," *American Bar Association Journal*, XLIX, No. 11 (November, 1963), 1089–91.

Hubatsch, W. "Die nordischen unionbestrebungen," *Zeitschrift für Geopolitik,* XXVI, No. 3 (March, 1955), 174–86.

"Inter-Scandinavian Co-operation," *External Affairs,* VII, No. 10 (October, 1955), 246–52.

Karjalainen, Ahti. "Plan for the Expansion and Improvement of Economic Co-operation in the Nordic Countries," *Bank of Finland Monthly,* XXXI, No. 12 (December, 1957), 18–21.

Kruse, Frederik Vinding. *A Nordic Draft Code.* Copenhagen: Munksgaard, 1963. Pp. xx, 412.

Lange, Halvard M. "The Northern Countries and Europe: Some Norwegian Viewpoints," *The Norseman,* VIII, No. 1 (January–February, 1950), 1–9.

————. "Scandinavian Cooperation in International Affairs," *International Affairs,* XXX, No. 3 (July, 1954), 285–93.

Larsen, Knud. "Die nordische zusammenarbeit auf dem Gebiete des Staatsangehörigkeitsrechts," *Le Nord,* IV, No. 1 (1942), 65–81.

Lindgren, Raymond E. "International Co-operation in Scandinavia," *Year Book of World Affairs 1959* (London: Stevens, 1959), XIII, 95–114.

————. *Norway-Sweden: Union, Disunion and Scandinavian Integration.* Princeton, N.J.: Princeton University Press, 1959. Pp. ix, 298.

Lund, Torben. "La Coopération Nordique dans le domaine du droit de propriété intellectuelle," *Le Nord,* III, No. 2–4 (1940), 112–28.

Lundgren, Nils. "Nordic Common Market—For and Against," *EFTA Bulletin,* VII, No. 2 (March, 1966), 1–7; No. 3 (April, 1966), 10–15.

Mannio, Niilo A. "La Collaboration internordique en matière de politique sociale," *Le Nord,* II, No. 2 (1939), 138–47.

Matteucci, Mario. "The Scandinavian Legislative Co-operation as a Model for European Co-operation," in *Liber Amicorum of Congratulations to Algot Bagge* (Stockholm: Norstedt, 1956), pp. 136–45.

Mead, W. R. "Scandinavianism and the Future of Scandinavia," *The Norseman,* I, No. 6 (November 1943), 438–43.

Meissner, Frank. "Scandinavian Customs Union," *The Norseman,* XII, No. 4 (July–August, 1954), 246–54.

Montgomery, Arthur. "From a Northern Customs Union to EFTA," *Scandinavian Economic History Review,* VIII, No. 1 (1960), 45–70.

Moritzen, Julius. "Scandinavian Renaissance," *Current History,* VIII, No. 44 (April, 1945), 330–35.

Nelson, Robert A. "Scandinavian Airlines System Cooperation in the Air," *Journal of Air Law and Commerce,* XX (1953), 178–96.

"Nordic Co-operation," *Current Notes on International Affairs,* XXXIII, No. 9 (September, 1962), 11–21.

Nordic Cooperation: Report on the Conference Organized by the Nordic Council for International Organizations in Europe. Stockholm: Kungl. Boktr., 1965. Pp. 127.

Nordic Co-operation in the Social and Labour Field. (Published under the auspices of the Nordic Committee on Social Policy.) Denmark: Rosenborg, 1965. Pp. 48.

Olsson, Bertil. "The Common Employment Market for the Northern Countries," *International Labour Review,* LXVIII, No. 4–5 (October–November, 1953), 364–74.

Orfield, Lester B. "Uniform Scandinavian Laws," *American Bar Association Journal,* XXXVIII, No. 9 (September, 1952), 773–75.

Padelford, Norman J. "Regional Cooperation in Scandinavia," *International Organization,* XI, No. 4 (Autumn, 1957), 597–614.

Pedersen, Poul Trier. "Four Nations Break Down the Barriers," *Danish Foreign Office Journal,* No. 14 (December, 1954), pp. 18–19.

Petrén, Gustaf. "Memorandum on the Problem of Method in Nordic Legislative Cooperation . . . ," *Unification du Droit/Unification of Law* (Rome: Unidroit, 1960), IX, 209–18.

————. "Les Résultats de Dix Ans de Coopération Nordique," *Annuaire Européen/European Yearbook* (The Hague: Nijhoff, 1965), XI, 27–43, with English summary, pp. 43–49.

————. "Scandinavian Cooperation," *Annuaire Européen/European Yearbook* (The Hague: Nijhoff, 1956), II, 60–75.

Pontoppidan, Niels. "A Mature Experiment: The Scandinavian Experience," *American Journal of Comparative Law,* IX (1960), 344–49.

Procopé, Hjalmar J. "Economic Co-operation Between the Northern Countries and the Joint Delegation for Its Promotion," *Le Nord,* I (1938), 48–58.

"Prospettive della collaborazione nordica," *Relazioni Internazionali,* XXII, No. 47 (Nov. 22, 1958), 1469–70.

Salvesen, Kaare. "Co-operation in Social Affairs Between the Northern Countries of Europe," *International Labour Review,* LXXIII, No. 4 (April, 1956), 334–57.

"Scandinavian Co-operation," *Current Notes on International Affairs,* XXVI, No. 3 (March, 1955), 156–63.

"Scandinavian Co-operation in Social Affairs," in George R. Nelson (ed.), *Freedom and Welfare* (Krohn: The Ministries of Social Welfare of Denmark, Finland, Iceland, Norway, and Sweden, 1953), pp. 485–96.

Seip, Helge. "The Pursuit of the Possible in Scandinavian Cooperation," *The Norseman,* XIV, No. 3 (May–June, 1956), 145–50.

Some Notes on the Scandinavian Market. Stockholm: Ervaco, 1963. Pp. 57.

Strahl, Ivar. "Les Congrès de juristes Nordiques," *Revue Internationale de Droit Comparé*, IV (1952), 259–67.

————. "Scandinavian Co-operation in the Field of Legislation," in Jørgen Bukdahl *et al.* (ed.), *Scandinavia Past and Present* (Odense: Arnkrone, 1959), III, 113–17.

————. "The Scandinavian Jurists' Congresses," in Jørgen Bukdahl *et al.* (ed.), *Scandinavia Past and Present* (Odense: Arnkrone, 1959), III, 118–21.

"The Union in Northern Europe," *Inter-Parliamentary Bulletin*, XLIV, No. 3 (1964), 86–90.

Wasberg, Gunnar Christie. "The Nordic Cultural Commission," *American-Scandinavian Review*, XLIX, No. 2 (June, 1961), 169–73.

————. "Scandinavian Unity: Common Interests Despite Divergencies," *The Norseman*, XXI, No. 2 (1963), 2–6.

Wendt, Frantz. "The Norden Association," *American-Scandinavian Review*, XLIV, No. 3 (September, 1956), 245–49.

————. ————, in Jørgen Bukdahl *et al.* (ed.), *Scandinavia Past and Present* (Odense: Arnkrone, 1959), III, 49–54.

————. "Nordic Cooperation—Past and Present," in J. A. Lauwerys (ed.), *Scandinavian Democracy* (Copenhagen: Schultz, 1958), pp. 370–88.

Wilhjelm, Johan. "Die Verhandlungen über einen gemeinsamen nordischen Markt," *Europa-Archiv*, XI, No. 18 (Sept. 20, 1956), 9171–74.

Wuorinen, John H. "Scandinavian Unity: Problems and Prospects," *American-Scandinavian Review*, XLV, No. 3 (September, 1957), 264–68.

Würtemberg, Erik Marks von. "Die gemeinsame nordische Gesetzgebung," *Zeitschrift für Ausländisches und Internationales Privatrecht*, X, No. 5–6 (1936), 705–23.

INDEX

Åland Islands, 141
Andrén, Nils, 106
Arab countries, 143
Asgeirsson, Asgeir, 6
Atomic Energy Questions, Consultative Committee on, 68, 117
Austria, 9

Baltic Sea, 3, 12
Belgium, 149
Benediktsson, Bjarni, 8
Benelux, 137, 148
Bjarnason, Sigurdur, 39
Bonsdorff, Göran von, 8
Borten, Per, 6
Bothnia, Gulf of, 3
Branders, Håkan, 114–15
Bratteli, Trygve, 39
Byström, Tryggve, 45

Cabinet government. *See* Parliamentarism
Cabinet members: joint meetings of Scandinavian, 110–12, 121; joint meetings with Nordic Council Presidium, 110, 120, 121
Canada, 143
Cassel, Leif, 38
Civil servants: exchange of, 70, 95; contact among, 112–13
Common market. *See* European Economic Community
Common Nordic labor market, 22, 23, 117, 139, 145
Common Nordic market negotiations, 64, 74, 75, 77, 95, 96, 112, 118, 119, 120, 125–39, 144; Swedish-Danish common market proposals, 126, 128
Consular coordination, 97, 145–46

Cooperation: defined, viii, 147
Copenhagen, 3, 17, 19, 20, 53, 54, 58, 137
Council of Europe, 32, 42, 89, 148

Dahlgaard, Bertel, 23n, 147
Dam, Peter Mohr, 141
Daylight saving time, 93–94

Eastern Europe, 11, 13
Edberg, Rolf, 21
Eriksen, Erik, 38, 73
Erlander, Tage, 5–6, 117–18, 120, 124n, 133
Euratom, 148
European Coal and Steel Community (ECSC), 108, 148
European Economic Community (EEC), 10, 12, 13, 18, 74, 119, 122, 123, 132, 135, 138, 144, 148, 149. *See also* Rome, Treaty of
European free trade area negotiations, 58, 115, 132, 133, 134
European Free Trade Association (EFTA), 11–12, 13, 19, 25, 74, 91, 96, 99, 119, 120, 123, 135, 137, 138, 139, 144, 146. *See also* FINEFTA

Faeroe Islands, 4, 141, 142
Fagerholm, Karl-August, 39, 123, 133
FINEFTA, 12. *See also* European Free Trade Association
Finland: relations with Soviet Union. *See* Soviet Union
Finnish accession to Nordic Council, 24, 103–4, 151, 152
Finno-Ugric, 4

Force, renunciation of use in Scandinavia, 136, 146
France, 4, 149
Freud, Sigmund, 144
Funen, 3

General Agreement on Tariffs and Trade (GATT), 74, 127, 138
Gerhardsen, Einar, 6, 39, 74–75, 133
Germany, 3, 4, 10, 11, 149
Great Britain, 4, 10, 11, 13–14, 18
Greenland, 4, 6, 141

Haas, Ernst, 146, 148
Hækkerup, Per, 136–37
Hambro, C. J., 12, 21
Hansen, H. C., 6, 24
Hansson, Per Albin, 5
Harpsund conference, 111, 121, 122, 135
Hedtoft, Hans, 6, 21, 23, 24–25, 38, 41, 55, 68, 117, 118, 122
Helsinki, 19, 58
Helsinki Agreement, 61, 64, 98, 119, 123–24, 145, 174–81
Herlitz, Nils, 23, 31, 38, 55, 70, 73
Higher education: coordination of, 74
Holland, 149
Holm, Chr. H., 121
Holstein, 9
Hønsvald, Nils, 39, 78
Hultin, Eiler, 41
Hungarian language. See Finno-Ugric
Hungarian uprising, 29

Inner-Six. See European Economic Community
Inter-Parliamentary Union, 15–16, 99. See also Nordic Inter-Parliamentary Union
Intoxication: presumptive, 93, 94
Italy, 4, 149

Johnsen, Håkon, 49–50
Joint Nordic Committee for Economic Cooperation, 113, 115, 125–27. See also Nordic Economic Cooperation Committee
Joint patent court proposal, 97
Jónsson, Emil, 121

Jutland, 3
Juvenile delinquency, 103

Kalmar Union, 140
Kampmann, Viggo, 6, 111, 121, 133
Kekkonen, Urho, 7, 98
Kennedy Round, 138. See also General Agreement on Tariffs and Trade
Kraft, Ole Bjørn, 21, 120
Krag, Jens Otto, 6
Kruse, Frederik Vinding, 116

Lange, Gunnar, 69
Lange, Halvard, 68, 147n
Languages: in Scandinavia, 3, 4, 8, 140–41, 142, 151; in the Nordic Council, 16, 35–36, 43, 62, 69, 83, 107, 112
Lapland, 70, 90, 142
Larsen, Aksel, 29, 99
Latin America, 143, 148
League of Nations, 141
Lindgren, Raymond E., 146
Little Europe. See European Economic Community
Løchen, Einar, 42
Lundgren, Nils, 138
Lutheranism, 5
Luxemburg, 107, 135, 149
Lyng, John, 39

Mead, W. R., 145
Meinander, Ragnar, 41
Middle East, 148
Ministries of Nordic Affairs: proposed, 121
Moscow, 4
Myrdal, Gunnar, 144

NATO, 10, 12, 13; Parliamentarians' Council, 42, 148
Nazi occupation, 9, 12
New York City, 4
Nielsen, Harald, 39
Nord, Erik, 42
Norden Societies, 41, 106, 118, 142–43
Nordic Council: public relations activities of, 16, 40; as pressure group, 22, 117–18, 120, 124; deputy delegates, 29, 30, 64, 79, 158; expenses, 40, 70, 101–3, 108,

155–56, 165; relations with national bureaucracies, 44, 46, 121, 122–23, 124; Prize in Music, 44–45; Literary Prize, 45; extraordinary sessions, 59, 153, 158; unanimity, 77–78, 84–85, 89, 90, 92–93, 95, 96, 99–100, 104, 109, 134–35, 136, 147

Nordic Council annual sessions: governmental participation, 40, 105–6; summoning, 56–59; introduction of matters, 60–73; governmental memoranda on past recommendations, 64–67, 106; reports on Scandinavian cooperation, 67–69, 106; supplementary proposals, 69; postponing matters, 71–72; preparing agendas, 72–73, 104–5; general debate, 73–77; reference to committee, 77–78; experts, role of, 79, 80, 81–82, 136, 170, 171; debate on second reading, 85–87; voting, 88–91, 163, 164; abstention, 90–91, 92, 94, 134, 155, 160; recommendations to governments, 91–101; closing a session, 100–101; exclusion of cold-war issues, 103–4

Nordic Council organs: secretariats, 16, 24, 40–46, 54–55, 107–8; Chief Clerk, Secretary of annual session, 26, 40–41, 73, 77, 83; national delegations, 26–33, 53–54; working committees, 33–36; joint working committees, 36–37, 53; Presidium, 37–40, 53–54, 69–71; President, 39–40; interim committees, 46–47, 49–51, 52–53, 58, 63–64, 104–5, 154; standing committees, 47–49, 78–85, 104–5; committee staff, 51–52

Nordic Cultural Commission, 41, 49, 113–15, 143

Nordic Cultural Fund, 97

Nordic Economic Cooperation Committee (NECC), 115–16, 128–31, 132, 133, 135, 137. See also Joint Nordic Committee for Economic Cooperation

Nordic Inter-Parliamentary Union (NIPU), 9, 15–17, 21, 24, 41, 103, 113, 118, 153; Statute, 182–84

Nordic investment bank: proposed, 136

Nordic Jurists: meetings of, 23

Nordic Ministerial Committee for Economic Cooperation, 18, 61, 111, 112, 115, 116, 119, 122, 128, 132, 135

Nordic Parliamentary Committee for Traffic Freedom, 21–23. See also Nordic Traffic Committee

Nordic passport union, ix, 22–23, 96, 145

Nordic Social Welfare Committee, 113, 115–16

Nordic Traffic Committee, 22, 50. See also Nordic Parliamentary Committee for Traffic Freedom

Nordic Uniform Law Committee, 116. See also Uniform laws

Nordvision, 76

Northrop, F. S. C., 143

Nuclear weapons prohibition: proposals for, 98–99, 104

Ohlin, Bertil, 38, 120

Organization for European Economic Cooperation (OEEC), 91, 134, 135

Oslo, 17, 53, 58

Outer-Seven. See European Free Trade Association

Paasikivi line, 11. See also Soviet Union: relations with Finland

Paasio, Rafael, 7

Pan-Scandinavian movement, 9, 136, 142

Paris Peace Treaty of 1947, 10. See also Soviet Union: relations with Finland

Parliamentarism, 5, 24

Patent court proposal. See Joint patent court proposal

Petrén, Gustaf, 42–43, 55

Pettersson, Anders, 85

Pitsinki, Kaarlo, 39

Political parties, 5–8, 18, 24, 29, 31, 34, 41, 47–48, 50, 51, 63, 75, 97, 104, 141; cross-national cohesion, 63, 69, 95, 98, 99; youth clubs, 80, 171

Population, 4, 137

Poulsen, Johan, 141

Proportional representation, 5, 26–29
Prussia, 9, 11
Public opinion on Nordic integration, 119–20

Regionalism: defined, viii, 8–9
Religion, 5, 139, 142. *See also* Lutheranism
Reykjavik, 58
Rome, Treaty of, 138. *See also* European Economic Community
Russia, 140, 141. *See also* Soviet Union
Russo-Finnish Treaty of 1948, 10–11. *See also* Soviet Union
Ryman, Sven-Hugo, 52

Salvesen, Kaare, 115
Scandinavian Airlines System (SAS), 138
Scandinavian Defense Alliance negotiations, 10, 12, 15, 17–19, 23, 103, 118, 125, 144
Scandinavian parliaments: joint meetings of committees from, 10, 15, 19–20
Scania, 3, 145
Schleswig, 3, 9, 142
Seip, Helge, 76–77
Sigurdsson, Fridjón, 41
Sigurdsson, Jón, 41
Sirén, Eino, 39
Skaug, Arne, 134
Social security: reciprocity, 22, 23, 145

Solheim, Bjarne, 42
The Sound, 3, 19, 90, 105, 145
Southeast Asia, 148
Soviet Union, 3, 8, 142; relations with Finland, 10–11, 12, 24, 91. *See also* Russia
Stauning, Thorvald, 6
Stockholm, 16, 20, 45, 46, 54, 58
Suicide, 144n
Sukselainen, V. J., 44, 122
Supranationality, 9, 12, 25, 54, 97, 107–8, 120, 146, 149
Swede-Finns, 41, 140–41
Switzerland, 143

Thestrup, Knud, 52

Unanimity. *See* Nordic Council
Undén, Östen, 68, 147
Underdeveloped nations: coordinating aid to, 74
Uniform laws, 19–20, 97, 116, 145
Union of Norden Societies. *See* Norden Societies
United Nations, 110

Virolainen, Johannes, 86

Wallmén, Olof, 43n, 45
Wendt, Frantz, 41, 43, 55
West Africa, 148
Wikborg, Erling, 89

Yugoslavia, 143

Zealand, 3

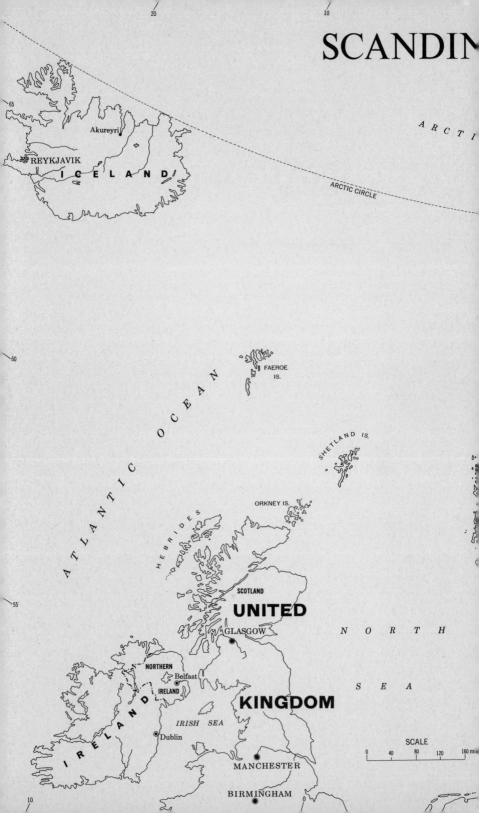

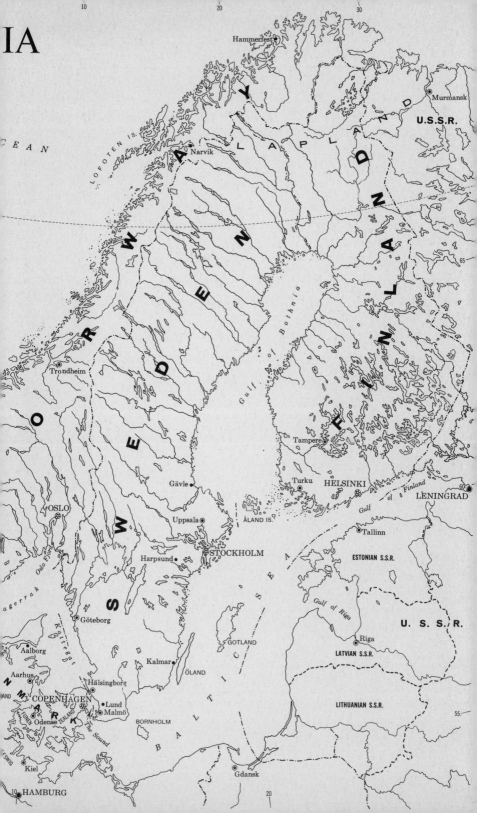

IA

Hammerfest

Murmansk

U.S.S.R.

OCEAN

LOFOTEN IS.

Narvik

L A P L A N D

N O R W A Y

Trondheim

S W E D E N

Gulf of Bothnia

F I N L A N D

Tampere

Gävle

Turku

HELSINKI

LENINGRAD

Gulf of Finland

OSLO

Uppsala

ÅLAND IS.

Oslo Fjord

Harpsund

STOCKHOLM

Tallinn

ESTONIAN S.S.R.

Skagerrak

Göteborg

B A L T I C   S E A

GOTLAND

Gulf of Riga

U. S. S. R.

Riga

LATVIAN S.S.R.

Kattegat

Aalborg

Kalmar

ÖLAND

Aarhus

Hälsingborg

DENMARK

COPENHAGEN

Lund

Malmö

BORNHOLM

LITHUANIAN S.S.R.

FUNEN

Odense

ZEALAND

The Sound

Kiel

Gdansk

HAMBURG